CONTENTS

Chapter One: Domestic Violence

Chapter Two: Abuse and Young People

Chapter Three: Tackling Abuse

Useful information for readers

Dear Reader,

Issues: Domestic Abuse

Domestic abuse affects over 350,000 people in England and Wales alone, but many myths still surround the issue. Some people do not realise that abuse does not mean only physical violence: it can also be verbal and emotional, and can impact seriously on any children present in the relationship in addition to the victim. This book looks at the impact of hidden domestic abuse on individuals and society.

The purpose of *Issues*

Domestic Abuse is the one hundred and fifty-fifth volume in the **Issues** series. The aim of this series is to offer up-to-date information about important issues in our world. Whether you are a regular reader or new to the series, we do hope you find this book a useful overview of the many and complex issues involved in the topic.

Titles in the **Issues** series are resource books designed to be of especial use to those undertaking project work or requiring an overview of facts, opinions and information on a particular subject, particularly as a prelude to undertaking their own research.

The information in this book is not from a single author, publication or organisation; the value of this unique series lies in the fact that it presents information from a wide variety of sources, including:

⇨ Government reports and statistics
⇨ Newspaper articles and features
⇨ Information from think-tanks and policy institutes
⇨ Magazine features and surveys
⇨ Website material
⇨ Literature from lobby groups and charitable organisations. *

Critical evaluation

Because the information reprinted here is from a number of different sources, readers should bear in mind the origin of the text and whether the source is likely to have a particular bias or agenda when presenting information (just as they would if undertaking their own research). It is hoped that, as you read about the many aspects of the issues explored in this book, you will critically evaluate the information presented. It is important that you decide whether you are being presented with facts or opinions. Does the writer give a biased or an unbiased report? If an opinion is being expressed, do you agree with the writer?

Domestic Abuse offers a useful starting point for those who need convenient access to information about the many issues involved. However, it is only a starting point. Following each article is a URL to the relevant organisation's website, which you may wish to visit for further information.

Kind regards,

Lisa Firth
Editor, **Issues** series

*Please note that Independence Publishers has no political affiliations or opinions on the topics covered in the **Issues** series, and any views quoted in this book are not necessarily those of the publisher or its staff.*

What is domestic violence?

Information from Women's Aid

There are a number of different definitions of domestic violence. In Women's Aid's view, domestic violence is physical, psychological, sexual or financial violence that takes place within an intimate or family-type relationship and forms a pattern of coercive and controlling behaviour. This can include forced marriage and so-called 'honour' crimes. Domestic violence often includes a range of abusive behaviours, not all of which are, in themselves, inherently 'violent' – hence some people prefer to use the term 'domestic abuse' rather than 'domestic violence'.

Domestic violence is very common: research shows that it affects one in four women in their lifetime. Two women a week are killed by their partners or former partners. All forms of domestic violence – psychological, financial, emotional and physical – come from the abuser's desire for power and control over an intimate partner or other family members. Domestic violence is repetitive and life-threatening, it tends to worsen over time and it destroys the lives of women and children.

Crime statistics and research show that domestic violence is gender specific – that is, it is most commonly experienced by women and perpetrated by men, particularly when there is a pattern of repeated and serious physical assaults, or when it includes rape or sexual assault or results in injury or death. Men can also experience violence from their partners (both within gay and straight relationships); however, women's violence towards men is often an attempt at self-defence, and is only rarely part of a consistent pattern of controlling and coercive behaviour. For this reason, we will generally refer to the abuser as 'he' and to the survivor as 'she'.

Domestic violence also has an

women's aid
until women & children are safe
www.womensaid.org.uk

enormous effect on the children in the family. Nearly three-quarters of children considered 'at risk' by Social Services are living in households where one of their parents/carers is abusing the other. A high proportion of these children are themselves being abused – either physically or sexually – by the same perpetrator. (Estimates vary between 30% to 66% depending upon the study.)

Any woman can experience domestic violence regardless of race, ethnic or religious group, class, disability or lifestyle. Domestic violence can also take place in lesbian, gay, bisexual and transgender relationships. Domestic violence can also be perpetrated by other family members (for example, extended family). In some cases, older children – teenagers or young adults – are violent or abusive towards their mothers or other family members.

Although every situation is unique, there are common factors that link the experience of an abusive relationship. Acknowledging these factors is an important step in preventing and stopping the abuse. This list can help you to recognise if you, or someone you know, are in an abusive relationship.

⇨ Destructive criticism and verbal abuse: shouting; mocking; accusing; name calling; verbally threatening.

⇨ Pressure tactics: sulking; threatening to withhold money, disconnecting the telephone, taking the car away, taking the children away, or reporting you to welfare agencies unless you comply with his demands; threatening or attempting suicide; withholding or pressuring you to use drugs or other substances; lying to your friends and family about you; telling you that you have no choice in any decisions.

⇨ Disrespect: persistently putting you down in front of other people; not listening or responding when you talk; interrupting your

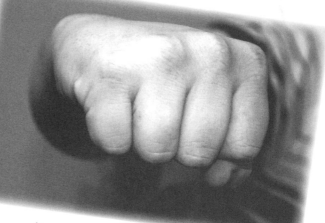

telephone calls; taking money from your purse without asking; refusing to help with childcare or housework.

⇨ Breaking trust: lying to you; withholding information from you; being jealous; having other relationships; breaking promises and shared agreements.

⇨ Isolation: monitoring or blocking your telephone calls; telling you where you can and cannot go; preventing you from seeing friends and relatives; shutting you in the house.

⇨ Harassment: following you; checking up on you; not allowing you any privacy (for example, opening your mail); repeatedly checking to see who has telephoned you; embarrassing you in public; accompanying you everywhere you go.

⇨ Threats: making angry gestures; using physical size to intimidate; shouting you down; destroying your possessions; breaking things; punching walls; wielding a knife or a gun; threatening to kill or harm you and the children; threatening to kill or harm family pets; threats of suicide.

⇨ Sexual violence: using force, threats or intimidation to make you perform sexual acts; having sex with you when you don't want it; forcing you to look at pornographic material; forcing you to have sex with other people; any degrading treatment related to your sexuality or to whether you are lesbian, bisexual or heterosexual.

⇨ Physical violence: punching; slapping; hitting; biting; pinching; kicking; pulling hair out; pushing; shoving; burning; strangling.

⇨ Denial: saying the abuse doesn't happen; saying you caused the abusive behaviour; being publicly gentle and patient; crying and begging for forgiveness; saying it will never happen again.

Is domestic violence a crime?

Domestic violence can include a number of different behaviours, and there is no single criminal offence of 'domestic violence'. Not all forms of domestic violence are illegal; some forms of emotional abuse, for example, are not defined as criminal – though these can also have a serious and lasting impact on a woman's or child's sense of well-being and autonomy.

However, many kinds of domestic violence constitute a criminal offence, including physical assault, wounding, attempting to choke, sexual assault, rape, threats to kill, harassment, stalking and putting people in fear of violence.

There is no excuse for domestic violence and the victim is never responsible for the abuser's behaviour

---

Who is responsible for the violence?

The abuser is always responsible for the violence, and should be held accountable. There is no excuse for domestic violence and the victim is never responsible for the abuser's behaviour.

'Blaming the victim' is something that abusers will often do to make excuses for their behaviour, and quite often they manage to convince their victims that the abuse is indeed their fault. This is part of the pattern and is in itself abusive. Blaming their behaviour on someone else, or on the relationship, their childhood, their ill health, or their alcohol or drug addiction is one way in which many abusers try to avoid personal responsibility for their behaviour.

It is important that any intervention to address domestic violence prioritises the safety of victims/survivors and holds the perpetrators accountable.

Women and men, victims and survivors

This article is primarily addressed to women for the following reasons:

⇨ The majority of domestic violence as defined above is perpetrated by men and experienced by women.

⇨ Women's Aid's information and support services exist to respond to the needs of women and children.

However, most of the information here would also apply equally to men who are on the receiving end of abuse, whether from a male or a female abuser.

The terms 'victim' and 'survivor' are both used, depending on the context. 'Survivor' is, however, preferred as it emphasises an active, resourceful and creative response to the abuse, in contrast to 'victim', which implies passive acceptance. If you are reading this, then you are – at least to some extent – a survivor.

References

⇨ Department of Health (2002) *Women's Mental health: Into the Mainstream: Strategic development of mental health care for women* (London: DH)

⇨ Farmer, E. and Pollack, S. (1998) *Substitute care for sexually abused and abusing children* (Chichester: Wiley)

⇨ Walby, Sylvia and Allen, Jonathan (2004) *Domestic violence, sexual assault and stalking: Findings from the British Crime Survey* (London: Home Office Research, Development and Statistics Directorate)

⇨ The above information is re-printed with kind permission from Women's Aid. Visit www.womensaid.org.uk for more information.

© Women's Aid

Myths and stereotypes

Information from End the Fear

There are many myths and stereotypes about domestic violence, which are untrue and often deeply unfair to the women who are suffering domestic violence. These attitudes, often from those who have no experience of domestic violence, can add to a woman's feelings of despair and isolation and make it more difficult for her to seek help. Here are some examples:

Q. Isn't domestic violence just all about hitting? Surely being emotionally abused isn't that bad?

A. People who have been abused in several ways often say that it was the emotional abuse that had the most effect on them. Being constantly undermined, criticised and humiliated can turn someone who was once confident and outgoing into a nervous, anxious person. The threat of being hit can be extremely controlling. But all violence and abuse is damaging and does not have to be tolerated.

Q. Don't some people choose violent partners or like the abuse? If not, why do they stay with them?

A. Nobody chooses a violent partner because they want to be abused. Abuse rarely starts at the beginning of the relationship and many people don't realise their partner's controlling behaviour might lead to violence. It can be hard to leave a partner if you live together or have children, who may love the other parent. Survivors of abuse often say they love their partner, but want the abuse to stop. They may think their partner can change. They may not know that what is going on is illegal and may not know about help available.

Q. Some women just go from one abusive relationship to another

A. Abusive men are not easy to identify. It's not easy to tell just by looking at somebody whether they are an abuser or not. In any event, at the beginning of relationships, men are often charming, attentive and caring. Although the majority of men are not, there are still very significant numbers of men who are abusers.

There is no correlation between a woman's background and the chances of her being abused.

Q. Don't some women provoke violence by their own behaviour?

A. Nobody deserves to be abused and there is no justification for violent crime. Domestic violence can happen to anyone – being 'a good wife/partner/mother' does not stop a woman being victimised.

What abusive men count as 'provocation' is abnormal: women are assaulted for not having a meal ready, or asking for money, or are attacked in their sleep. Provocation is an excuse offenders use to avoid responsibility for their behaviour. No woman ever deserves to be beaten, or abused, no matter what she has said or done. Often, no provocation is apparent, e.g. women asleep are assaulted or dragged out of bed. The idea that provocation leads to violence does not universally apply – if an abuser feels provoked by his boss or bank manager, it is unlikely that he would punch them in the face or kick them to the ground.

The biggest risk factor for suffering domestic violence is being a woman. Domestic violence does not just happen to bad people. Being good does not stop a woman being victimised. Abusers are not out of control and can choose to walk away if their partner is upsetting them or they feel they are being wound up by a situation.

Q. If domestic violence is that bad, why wouldn't they speak up or leave?

A. People experiencing domestic violence remain silent for many valid reasons. In the early stages, women often hope that the abuser will change or stop the violence. When it doesn't stop, a woman remains silent primarily because of fear: of the abuser's threats to kill her, to stalk her, to take her children away, to hurt others she loves, to kill her pet, to kill himself. It takes great courage to tell someone if a woman knows she will be at greater risk (often a valid assumption, based on past experience). She may not know where to go for help; she may be afraid of what he will do if she were to leave or if he were to find her. She may have been told she cannot take the children away from their father; she may hope he is going to change; she

may be under pressure from her family or community to stay. Sometimes the perpetrator has convinced her the abuse was her fault.

Q. He was abused himself: men who abuse women come from violent families

A. We know that many men who grow up in violent families don't go on to become abusers and many men who are violent to their partner come from families with no history of abuse. This myth is an excuse to let abusers blame their violence on their upbringing and not take responsibility for their behaviour. Just because he might have experienced abuse as a child this does not justify his behaviour. Each man has a choice.

Q. He has poor impulse control; a problem in anger management

A. Most domestic violence is systematic and premeditated, not a momentary loss of self-control. Many people feel angry but do not assault another person. Anger is a healthy feeling; physical violence is a criminal behaviour. In addition sexual violence, emotional, psychological and financial abuse cannot be explained by a 'loss of temper'. Most men who physically assault their partners do so in the privacy of their own home, not outside in public view, suggesting that his assaults are not subject to his current emotion or poor impulse control; he can wait to beat her when they get home, in a planned way. Some women are hauled out of bed when they are asleep and beaten.

The abuse is often directed to parts of the body that will not be visible if bruised. Most violent men would not attack their boss, bank manager or a stranger when frustrated or angry. If they have enough control to do this, they could use their control to walk away. His assault is often 'in cold blood' with no sign of 'loss of temper'. Physical assault may stop immediately if there is an interruption such as a phone call, a ring at the door, or if someone walks in.

Q. Black men are more violent to women because of their own experience of racist oppression and violence

A. Black men do face racist oppression but the statistics show violence is not greater within any ethnic minority group. Chauvinist views and oppression of women exist in all cultures, although gender power may be displayed in different ways.

Q. Asian women are passive and conform to male dominated culture and religion with harsh traditions (that may include wife beating, maiming and killing)

A. Women from different cultures experience domestic violence, and the risk does not differ significantly according to ethnicity or religion. Women who are Christian, Hindu, Jewish, Muslim and Sikh experience domestic violence. There is not such a thing as one Asian culture and the view that domestic violence is acceptable in Muslim communities is false and unsubstantiated. However, forced marriage, family honour (izzat) and shame (sharam) can play an important part in some Asian families and further limit women's ability and safety to seek help; Asian women are 2-3 times more likely to attempt suicide than other women.

Q. Drunks are violent; if he stopped drinking the domestic violence would stop

A. Many men who drink are not violent. Many men are sober when they abuse their partners and the majority of abusers are not alcoholics, and the majority of men classified as high level drinkers do not abuse their partners. Some men use drink to deny responsibility and as an excuse for violence; many women know before a perpetrator starts drinking that he will be violent. Women are 17 times more likely to contact police when a perpetrator is drunk or drugged because he is less predictable: contributing to a misconception that drugs or alcohol caused the violence.

Q. He's a good dad, so she should stay for the sake of the children

A. In 50-70% of homes where men assault women, children are abused as well. Half the men who abuse their wives assault their children more than twice a year. The impact of domestic violence is serious and cumulative. Witnessing domestic violence can cause a variety of physical, behavioural and emotional problems for children. Research shows the emotional and physical health of children improves considerably when they are removed from violence.

Q. It's just a tiff, domestic violence is a private matter; we shouldn't interfere

A. Domestic violence almost always is repeated and escalates in severity and frequency over time. Repeated abuse is damaging and potentially life-threatening to women and children. Domestic violence is purposeful and systematic behaviour that occurs without a two-sided argument, since victims learn not to answer back. Women are no more responsible than the victim of any other crime. Although some women fight back or defend themselves when they are being assaulted, this does not mean that she 'is as bad as him'.

Domestic violence of any kind is serious, causes significant injury and can be life-threatening. Many women have been killed 'accidentally' when their throat has been squeezed 'too hard' or when their head bounces off a wall for the last time. A 'row' does not mean injury or bodily harm.

Domestic violence is not something to be minimised nor is it just a private matter. Violence is a crime in society and a public matter. Domestic violence affects women and children, neighbours, family, friends, colleagues and communities. If we suspect a woman is experiencing domestic violence, we should try and let her know that we are there to support her. Focusing on the relationship clouds the issues and excuses the perpetrator. Women experiencing domestic violence very rarely exaggerate; indeed, the majority minimise and under-report the extent of the violence.

Q. There is no point in getting involved because the women always go back

A. Leaving violent situations does not guarantee safety. Women are at most risk of life-threatening violence when they attempt to leave or have recently left a partner. So leaving can be a very hard and frightening thing to do and women need support and help to do so in safety.

Q. What about the men abused by women?
A. Although domestic violence mainly affects women any man has the right to access support too. See section on men as victims.

Q. She stays/returns because she loves him or she is co-dependent
A. Loving the 'charmer' at the beginning is not the same as loving the reality: that the same person is capable of love and abuse. Women try many strategies to prevent abuse, and always hope it will never happen again. Women feel horror, terror, and disgust – and never talk of any positive features about being attacked. If a woman returns to a relationship, it is not to the violence that she is returning but to the hope that it has stopped.

Q. Some women just say they've

been abused to get re-housed
A. Leaving an abusive relationship can often mean leaving belongings and pets behind, taking children away from their father, friends and schools; living in overcrowded refuges or hostel accommodation while waiting for up to two years to be re-housed. Moving away from familiar surroundings, family, friends and community networks is something few women would choose to put themselves and their children through without good reason.

Q. Men who assault their wives are mentally ill
A. Woman abuse is too common to be explained or excused by mental illness. Most men with mental health problems do not abuse, and most abusers would not be diagnosed as mentally ill. The proportion of abusers who are mentally ill is no higher than in society as a whole. Even if it was caused by mental illness, why doesn't the abuser attack their employer, or strangers? Finally, trying to understand

him or his intent will not diminish the effects or impact of the violence on the victim, and her children.

Q. Men who beat their wives are a danger to the community
A. Perpetrators of domestic violence seldom attack anyone outside their family. The deterrents from attacking a stranger are much more established in law. The hidden nature of the secret increases her isolation and self-blame. However, indirectly, the repercussions of domestic violence do affect society: including the police, the courts, medical costs, education, employment and human rights. Domestic violence is against the law.

Q. It was a one-off. He's learned a lesson. He was really sorry
A. Domestic violence is not a single incident, or even a series of them. It is a systematic pattern of control and intimidation. Apologies may be another form of coercion, without evidence that he has taken responsibility for his abuse and means to keep his promise. On the whole, studies show that violence tends to recur and become more frequent and severe over time and domestic violence rarely stops without intervention.

Q. If my mum had a relationship with a violent man, does this make me more likely to become an abuser or victim?
A. No. If you are abused as a child this definitely doesn't mean that you are going to end up in a violent or abusive relationship yourself. Some research seems to show the opposite. Seeing what their parent went through means some people know what the effects are first-hand and never want to put anyone else through this. Others have found that through seeing the bad side of relationships they have learnt what to look out for. If you have any worries about this, you may want to talk to a friend, relative or counsellor.

⇨ The above information is reprinted with kind permission from End the Fear. Visit www.endthefear.org.uk for more information.
© End the Fear

How common is domestic abuse?

The prevalence of domestic abuse

Domestic abuse has been reported to affect over 350,000 people in England and Wales alone. Recently reported annual figures show 45,796 such incidents in Scotland, and 8,565 in Northern Ireland. It has been estimated that as many as approximately half a million older people are being abused at any one time in the United Kingdom (UK). The majority of perpetrators of elder abuse are family members.

No accurate figures exist for the prevalence of domestic abuse in all its forms, as it is known to be grossly under-reported to authorities, such as the police, health service and social services.

The British Crime Survey (BCS) found that 34 per cent of women, and 62 per cent of men who had suffered domestic abuse since they were 16 years of age have probably never told anyone other than the survey in question.

Indicators of socio-economic status show that there is increased prevalence of domestic abuse in areas associated with relatively lower levels of socio-economic status. Domestic abuse can, however, also occur within professional families, and this includes healthcare professionals themselves.
June 2007

⇨ The above information is reprinted with kind permission from the British Medical Association, and is taken from their report *Domestic abuse*, a BMA publication from the Board of Science. Visit www.bma.org.uk for more information or to view the full document.
© BMA

FAQs: why doesn't she leave?

Information from Women's Aid

Whilst the risk of staying may be very high, simply leaving the relationship does not guarantee that the violence will stop. In fact, the period during which a woman is planning or making her exit, is often the most dangerous time for her and her children.

Frequently, men who will become violent do not reveal this aspect of their behaviour until the relationship has become well established

Many women are frightened of the abuser, and with good reason. It's common for perpetrators to threaten to harm or even kill their partner or children if she leaves.

Reasons why a woman may not be ready to leave

⇨ She may still care for her partner and hope that they will change (many women don't necessarily want to leave the relationship, they just want the violence to stop).

⇨ She may feel ashamed about what has happened or believe that it is her fault.

⇨ She may be scared of the future (where she will go, what she will do for money, whether she will have to hide forever and what will happen to the children).

⇨ She may worry about money, and supporting herself and her children.

⇨ She may feel too exhausted or unsure to make any decisions.

⇨ She may be isolated from family or friends or be prevented from leaving the home or reaching out for help.

⇨ She may not know where to go.

⇨ She may have low self-esteem as a result of the abuse.

⇨ She may believe that it is better to stay for the sake of the children (e.g. wanting a father for her children and/or wishing to prevent the stigma associated with being a single parent).

Women and children need to know that they will be taken seriously and that their rights will be enforced. They need to have accessible options and be supported to make safe changes for themselves and their children. Resources and support they will need to leave safely include: money, housing, help with moving, transport, ongoing protection from the police, legal support to protect her and the children, a guaranteed income and emotional support. If a woman is not sure if these are available to her, this may also prevent her from leaving.

Women may also seek support from family or friends and the quality of the support they receive is likely to have a significant influence on their decision-making. Sometimes women will make several attempts to leave before they actually leave permanently and safely. Regardless of her decision, it is important that the support a woman receives enables her to increase her and her children's safety regardless of the choices she makes about her relationship to the abuser.

It also is vitally important that women are also supported whilst living with an abuser. If she feels that she will be excluded from ongoing support if she does not leave, she is unlikely to seek help from the same person or organisation again.

How important is specialist support when a woman tries to leave?

Access to culturally specific or specialised support may also be an important consideration for women from BME communities, lesbians, disabled women, asylum seekers and women with an insecure immigration status. These women often face additional barriers to seeking help in the first place – such as physical barriers, language, poverty and discrimination. Specialised help and a range of mechanisms to make contact and receive support are available via Women's Aid and throughout the England-wide network of domestic violence services.

What happens when family or friends try to help a woman leave?

Women may reach out to friends or family for help. When they do so, they can experience a variety of responses, ranging from the helpful to the utterly dangerous. However well-intended their help, friends or family may simply not know how to deal with the situation and may not be aware of the professional support and the legislative rights available.

Do women choose violent men?

Women do not seek out relationships with violent men. Frequently, men who will become violent do not reveal this aspect of their behaviour until the relationship has become well established. In fact, for many women, the violence does not start until their first pregnancy.

The first incident of domestic violence occurred after one year or more for 51% of the women surveyed; between three months and one year for 30%; between one and three months for 13% and under one month for 6% of women (Walby & Allen, 2004).

Amongst a group of pregnant women attending primary care in East London, 15% reported violence during their pregnancy; just under 40% reported that violence started whilst they were pregnant, whilst 30% who reported violence during pregnancy also reported they had at some time suffered a miscarriage as a result (Coid, 2000).

Are women who experience domestic violence 'helpless'?

'Learned helplessness' is an outdated concept in relation to our current understanding of domestic violence. It is a psychological theory that initially arose from animal behaviour research and was popular in the 1970s and 1980s.

In a recent study, researchers Dobash and Dobash said: 'The women in this study were also found to be actively engaged in trying to deal with violence and seeking outside assistance with these efforts. These women were neither helpless nor hopeless. While they did speak of the negative effects of living with violence, most had considerable strengths and held many positive views about themselves despite the harm and denigration they had suffered' (Dobash & Dobash, 2000).

Women living with and leaving violent men say that they want the violence to stop and are often actively engaged in trying to protect themselves and their children from it. They may also try a number of ways to cope with or get the violence to stop, including changing their own behaviour e.g. avoiding certain situations or appeasing the abuser by complying with his demands.

Key statistics: Why don't women leave?

⇨ Embarrassment and shame: A recent survey revealed that whilst 20% of women admit they have lived, or do currently live in fear of violence happening, more than half (52%) told researchers they'd be too embarrassed and ashamed to tell their friends, and 59% said they would not tell their families (YouGov, 2004).

⇨ Risk of homicide: Women are at greatest risk of homicide at the point of separation or after leaving a violent partner (Lees, 2000).

⇨ Effect on children: 60% of the women in the 'Routes to Safety' study left the abuser because they feared that they would be killed if they stayed. A further 54% of women left the abuser because they said that they could see that the abuse was affecting their children. 'In fact, 25% of the women said that they feared for their children's lives' (Humphreys & Thiara, 2002).

⇨ Effect of leaving: The British Crime Survey found that, while for the majority of women leaving the violent partner stopped the violence, 37% said it did not. For 18%, of those that had left their partner, they were further victimised by stalking and other forms of harassment. 7% of those that left said that the worst incident of domestic violence took place after they stopped living with their partner (Walby & Allen, 2004).

⇨ Post-separation violence: 76% of separated women reported suffering post-separation violence in the 'Routes to Safety' study. Of these women:
↳ 76% were subjected to continued verbal and emotional abuse.
↳ 41% were subjected to serious threats towards themselves or their children.
↳ 23% were subjected to physical violence.
↳ 6% were subjected to sexual violence.
↳ 36% stated that this violence was ongoing.

⇨ Child contact arrangements: In addition to this, more than half of those with post-separation child contact arrangements with an abusive ex-partner continued to have serious, ongoing problems with this contact (Humphreys & Thiara, 2002).

⇨ Contact with outreach services: 46% of the women in the 'Routes to Safety' study contacted outreach services for the first time when they were still living with their abuser; 90% of these women had since left the abuser (Humphreys & Thiara, 2002).

⇨ The above information is re-printed with kind permission from Women's Aid. Visit www.womensaid. org.uk for more information.
© Women's Aid

Domestic abuse – my story

Information from Lone Parents

When I was 22 a friend of my mother's came to stay with us after her abusive husband had thrown her out of the family home. After a few days she decided to return against the advice of my parents and myself. I remember desperately struggling to persuade her not to return and found it impossible to understand why she would so willingly go back to such a violent situation. If my partner had attempted to strangle me or threatened to take my child away from me I would not return to him and I am sure as you are reading this you are nodding your head in agreement. Surely no one in their right mind would do such a thing!

A year later while doing my last year at university I met a charming, well-travelled older man. My friends and family thought he was lovely. He was the kind of person who would do anything for anyone from giving old ladies a lift to the shops to doing odd jobs for a physically disabled friend. His family were equally fond of me and when a year later we announced that we were expecting a baby the champagne flowed!

From the heading at the top of this page you can guess this idyllic scenario did not last. I cannot say exactly when things started to go wrong; it is

difficult to remember now eight years on and to be quite honest I prefer to keep it that way. Some things are best forgotten. What I do remember is that the changes were subtle. Slowly he cut me off from my friends and restricted contact with my family. When I went out on my own I would be given a time to return home and to make sure I adhered to his wishes he would phone me to make sure I was leaving at the specified time. Once ill health forced me to give up work early in the pregnancy I became financially reliant on him and we spent more and more time with his doting parents. He chipped away at my confidence with constant criticism and by publicly humiliating me in front of my friends and family.

As the pregnancy continued he began to drink heavily and it was then that the rows started. I knew that something was not right but I could not admit it out loud, not even to myself, to do so would be to admit that I had made a dreadful mistake or worse ... that I had failed. One day while he was walking his dog I bundled my clothes into a bin liner and decided to leave. He returned just as I was opening the boot of my dilapidated old mini and begged me not to leave but to return to the flat and talk things through. As soon as

the front door was closed another row erupted as he taunted me for attempting to run away. I remember him knocking me on to the sofa and threatening to 'hunt me down' if I ever tried to leave again. From that moment on there would be more pushing and shoving. And more threats.

> **Domestic violence is not just about physical abuse, it is about living in fear without any control over your life and feeling isolated and powerless**

For a short time after the birth of our daughter it seemed that some semblance of normality might slip into our relationship. Photos were taken of a loving father with his arm wrapped protectively around the mother of his treasured child. Her christening was celebrated and he played the part of the attentive host but once the doors were closed and the novelty had passed the threats and the bruises returned with a vengeance. His heavy drink led to him being banned from driving and dependent on me for transport. This was a severe blow to his macho ego and he took out his frustration by constantly criticising my driving, telling me I was useless and that I was doing everything wrong.

He turned to drugs in order to keep up with the amount of building work he was receiving. As if his growing dependency on alcohol was not enough. He developed mood swings, erratic behaviour and rarely slept at night. He spent increasing amounts of money on his substance abuse leaving less for household bills and expenses and for his family.

One night when our daughter was 14 months old, he decided to wake me up on the hour every hour until

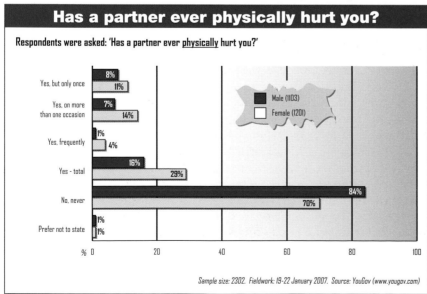

Has a partner ever physically hurt you?

Respondents were asked: 'Has a partner ever physically hurt you?'

Male (1103)
Female (1201)

	Male	Female
Yes, but only once	8%	11%
Yes, on more than one occasion	7%	14%
Yes, frequently	1%	4%
Yes - total	16%	29%
No, never	84%	70%
Prefer not to state	1%	1%

Sample size: 2302. Fieldwork: 19-22 January 2007. Source: YouGov (www.yougov.com)

6am. Three hours, later I took our child to her first session of 'mothers and toddlers'. The room was filled with happy children accompanied by chatting mothers who appeared to live 'normal' lives. I so wanted to be one of them yet the thought of one of these women visiting my home for a cup of coffee filled me with dread. As I walked home I decided something had to be done but I had no idea what. Who should I turn to for help, the Samaritans? The kind of people who contacted them were suicidal, desperate people, my problems were trivial by comparison and I had no right to waste their time with my problems. I phoned my parents and tearfully told them everything. Three days later while he was out visiting a friend my parents came round with a police escort to pack our clothes and my daughter's toys. Suddenly I felt as if I could breathe again.

When he phoned my parents to ask if they knew where I was he gave no hint that there was anything wrong with our relationship and even asked my father out for a drink! Once he realised I had left his tactics changed. His family started to phone me to tell me he was in such a state. His friends called to ask me what was wrong – when I told them what had happened behind closed doors they began telling me about former girlfriends of his who had left him suddenly. Day after day I was bombarded with phone calls and letters from him pleading with me to go back. His parents told me they had called in a 'crisis team' because he had become suicidal and that he had been referred to a counsellor for his addictions.

Well-meaning friends gave me well-meaning advice and eager encouragement not to go back. My parents made suggestions about new living arrangements and how my daughter could be cared for while I returned to work. It seemed to me that once again my life was being mapped out for me, while I was living in fear that some day soon he would carry out his threats to snatch our daughter or to attack my parents. No one seemed to understand my fears, instead they were trivialised, 'oh he's all talk, he wouldn't dare!' Yet those fears were real enough for me to dread going out

and to lie awake at night wondering what the future held or if there even was a future. I could not eat or sleep and I felt as if I was standing on the edge of a precipice waiting for a gentle breeze to send me tumbling down into the darkness.

After six weeks I wanted it all to stop and the pain to go away. I wanted to know where he was and what vengeance he was planning. There was only one way to do this.

I went back.

I knew my friends and family would not understand why but I found numerous ways to justify what I was doing. I worked hard to convince them – and myself – that what I was doing was for the best.

When I went back he promised never to take drugs again and to cut down on his drinking. He suggested we moved nearer to his parents so that he would no longer have any contact with friends that might tempt him back to his old ways and we began looking for a house. He paid a deposit on our first holiday abroad and bought clothes and gifts for our daughter and me. The man that I had fallen in love with almost three years before was back and life was sweet once more.

Less than a month later I knew I had walked back into a trap. He quickly turned back to his old ways without the help of any of his friends. This time the threats were far more sinister as he went into detail about how he would kill me and destroy my family. The abuse grew constant as did the rows but this time leaving would be far more difficult as he watched me closer than ever before.

As we moved far from the support of my worried friends and family one piece of well-meaning advice stuck in my mind. My mother's friend had by now moved back to her home town, far from her abusive ex-husband. She had suggested that I went into a refuge for women fleeing domestic violence. At the time I had dismissed her advice. Why would I go into a refuge? I was not suffering from domestic violence. He had never hit me; sure I had bruises but nothing more!

Trapped in a relationship that was growing ever worse, the notion

of domestic violence began to grow in my mind. Every time I saw leaflets on the subject I would secretly take one to read during my rare moments of privacy. As I read the various descriptions of domestic violence one message glared out at me from all the others:

domestic violence is not just about physical abuse, it is about living in fear without any control over your life and feeling isolated and powerless.

Armed with this knowledge I found the determination to do something about my situation.

By now our arguments were a daily occurrence. On one occasion I walked out of the house cradling our hysterical daughter while he yelled insults at me. As she was getting older I knew I had to do something before she started suffering from the consequence of my own failure to act. Nine months after we had returned to him I came home from shopping to find evidence of his return to drugs. That was the last straw. Four days later I pretended to take our daughter to her mother and toddler group. I walked around the back of the hall, out into the street behind it and straight into town to the Social Services department.

I gave the duty officer a letter in which I had written down everything I could think of that he had either done to me or threatened me with including what had happened in front of our two-year-old daughter. The social worker phoned a refuge to arrange somewhere for us to stay and phoned a solicitor to give me immediate advice on my rights. This time I was determined to remain in control. When the social worker told me she had arranged for us to go straight to a refuge I refused to go immediately. We had done nothing wrong, why should we be forced to leave all our possessions behind and go with only the clothes we were wearing? The refuge agreed to keep the room open for me for another two days. Those two days were to be the longest I have ever known. While he played in a pool tournament I packed our clothes and a few possessions in bin liners which I hid in the garage. On 9th July 1998 at 1.15pm my daughter and I left by taxi to begin our new lives.

Domestic violence in all its forms is devastating but you are not alone and you are not powerless

---

We stayed in two refuges; the first was run by Women's Aid and the second by a housing association. In both refuges we found women who had been through similar experiences and who supported each other in such a low point in their lives. Both offered counselling and advice on housing and benefits. My daughter met her first 'best friend' in the second refuge. I met some very good friends in both.

For me being a single parent is bliss. Compared to the life we had before this is easy! Sure there have been some bad times when I have felt very low but I have never been as low as I was before I left my daughter's father. No matter how bad things get I know I can cope because I have coped with worse.

If you are in an abusive relationship I hope you can find some inspiration from my experience. Domestic violence in all its forms is devastating but you are not alone and you are not powerless. The first step to regaining control over your life is recognising what is wrong.

Domestic violence is not just physical abuse. It can be emotional, psychological and sexual abuse.

I saw over forty women go through the doors of the second refuge and very few of them had any signs of physical injury yet most were terrified of their abusive partners.

Advice and support

Although physical injuries can heal within days, weeks or even months psychological and emotional scars can take years to heal. Depression, panic and anxiety attacks, eating disorders, flashbacks, sleeping problems, nightmares and behavioural problems in children are all common after leaving an abusive relationship. If you have any worries or concerns about your or your child's physical or mental health you need to see your doctor or health visitor. Do not suffer in silence because there is no shame in asking for help and we all need it at some point in our lives.

If you are concerned about the long-term effects of abuse for yourself and your children see counselling and support for information on finding a counsellor and support for you and your children.

If you need legal advice the Citizens' Advice Bureau is a good place to visit and they will also offer advice on housing and benefits you can find their contact details in the section: useful information. This section also includes contact details for the Samaritans, BT (British Telecommunications) malicious calls helpline and Voice UK.

⇨ The above information is reprinted with kind permission from Lone Parents. For more information on this and other issues, visit www.lone-parents.org.uk

Domestic abuse 'epidemic' affects 8m

More than eight million people are victims of domestic abuse, the British Medical Association reported yesterday.

Its study estimated that three in 10 women and one in five men suffer the problems, while 750,000 children routinely witness it.

But the experts said that the figures are likely to be 'grossly underestimated'.

Domestic abuse costs the country more than £3 billion a year. The report said that physical and psychological abuse has become a major health problem leading to heart attacks and mental illness. It calls for a Government-funded refuge building programme to deal with it.

Yesterday, doctors said all women who visit hospital A&E departments suffering injuries should be questioned to find out if they are victims.

Prof Vivienne Nathanson, of the BMA, said: 'The figures we provide in this report are shocking, but perhaps more alarming is that they are likely to be grossly underestimated.'

Prof Gene Feder, the report's author, said: 'If domestic violence was an infectious illness we would be calling it an epidemic. It is having a real impact on public health.

'I would say that any woman who attends A&E with an injury should be asked if they are victims of domestic abuse.'

Prof Nathanson added: 'Children need to understand what abuse is. It needs to be de-normalised so they understand that what they are seeing is aberrant behaviour that they can do something about.

'Children brought up in abusive households are often caught up in abuse as adults, either as victims or aggressors. The purpose of education is to try and break the cycle.'

The report also said doctors should be on the front line tackling the problem because surveys show they are the first people victims turn to.

21 June 2007

Pregnant, but not immune from violence

Recent research has shown that domestic violence towards a woman might begin or escalate during her pregnancy. By Josa Young

A hidden crime

When Dr Susan Bewley, clinical director of Guy's and St Thomas's Hospitals, came across US research into domestic violence during pregnancy, she decided the issue needed to be addressed in the UK. 'We knew about the occasional case of abuse and violence – but once we started looking, we simply found more,' she says.

One US study showed that 37 per cent of obstetric patients were suffering abuse, and that 30 per cent of domestic violence actually started during pregnancy. Domestic abuse was identified as a major health issue for pregnant women: a Yale study revealed that abused women were 15 times more likely to suffer a miscarriage.

Accessing abused pregnant women

Together with US criminologist Betsy Stanko, of the Economic and Social Research Council (ESRC), Dr Bewley designed a research programme to examine the issue of domestic violence in pregnancy. The study's objectives were to find out whether domestic violence commonly began or intensified during pregnancy and after the baby was born.

Their worst fears were realised – of the 892 women who participated in the study, 22 reported domestic violence in the course of the current pregnancy. The lifetime prevalence of domestic violence detected during research was 13.4 per cent. In the year before the study, only one case of domestic violence had been detected, and that was because the woman was admitted to A&E.

Acceptable questioning

The abuse was only revealed when midwives asked the right questions. Women are reluctant to admit to abuse without prompting. They feel embarrassed and ashamed, and often think that they are to blame. Partners accompany some women, which further inhibits disclosure.

A crucial element of the study was to find out how acceptable questioning about domestic violence was. Midwives were trained to ask particular questions, and the responses they received were examined to assess effectiveness. This screening was done as part of normal antenatal care at first booking, at 34 weeks and within the 10-day post-partum period.

Regardless of how they responded, all the women were handed information about refuges and contact numbers for police domestic violence teams. Information was also posted up in the clinic lavatories. Before the study started, a support team of social workers, interpreters and other specialists was put together to back up the midwives.

The vast majority of mothers were happy to take part. Women were more than six times more likely to disclose violence than if they were left to mention it without being prompted. Many of them said it was a relief at last to be able to tell someone, and that it made them think about making changes to their lives.

Domestic violence as a risk factor for pregnancy

Violence in pregnancy is a serious healthcare issue. Women victims are far more likely to describe their pregnancies as unplanned and unwanted. Abused pregnant women are at increased risk of miscarriage, infection, pre-term labour, placental abruption and low-birth-weight babies. This is obviously in addition to serious physical and mental problems for the woman herself including substance abuse and non-attendance for antenatal care.

The most recent *Confidential Enquiries in Maternal Death* – a document prepared every three years by the Department of Health – acknowledged domestic violence as a cause of maternal death for the first time.

The report recommended that, 'A sensitive enquiry about domestic violence should be routinely included when taking a social history (during pregnancy). Ideally this information should be sought in the absence of the woman's partner. Advice or information about local sources of help should be available.'

Why does it happen?

According to Betsy Stanko, 'Domestic violence is all about power and control.' The man will suspect that his partner's attention is elsewhere, and these feelings might become uncontrollable, leading to a violent response. This can intensify after delivery as the woman's relationship with her baby becomes more concrete.

'That concentration on the baby vital for the survival of the species takes the woman's attention away from the man, which can lead to the man losing control,' says Dr Bewley.

Help is at hand

A pregnant woman suffering from domestic violence can be accessed more easily than other abused women, because virtually 100 per cent pass through the health service.

'Her life changes when she becomes pregnant,' says Dr Bewley. 'And we have the opportunity to change her life.'

⇨ The above information is reprinted with kind permission from iVillage UK. Visit www.iVillage.co.uk for more information.

Male victims of domestic violence

Whether you are male or female, the definition of domestic violence is the same. TheSite.org uncovers the hidden abuse that affects many young men

Although research shows that domestic violence affects mostly women, current statistics show that one in six men will be affected at some point in their lifetime. The British Crime Survey revealed that 19% of domestic violence incidents were reported to be male victims, with just under half of these having a female abuser.

Abuse is experienced in many different ways and can include a range of physical, sexual, psychological or financial behaviour. Domestic violence is about power and control and is rarely a one-off incident. Violence usually takes place within an intimate relationship, such as a partner or a family member, and forms a pattern of controlling behaviour where the abuser tries to control and seek power over their victim.

Jason, 24, was married to his wife for two years, having been together for six years in total: 'She used to scream at me all the time and lash out during arguments. I had to tell colleagues that the cat was always scratching me. Really it was my wife, but I couldn't tell them that. How could I tell my mates? How could I just drop that into the conversation?'

Is it different for men?

Being abused by somebody you love and trust can be confusing and bewildering. The emotions you feel as a result are going to be similar whether you are male or female, however, it can be harder for men to cope with the emotional impact of domestic abuse. A spokesperson from the Men's Advice Line says: 'We often have men on the phone who say they can cope with the odd slap, but being constantly criticised and belittled is harder to deal with.'

We all know that women love a good natter, and while admitting to

By Liz Scarff

being abused is difficult for anybody, men often don't have the social networks in place to easily tell a friend or family member. When guys go down the pub it is not necessarily for a touchy-feely chat. Phone lines, like the Men's Advice Line (MALE), will give you the opportunity to talk in confidence.

It's happening to me

Being assaulted by somebody you know is just as much a crime as being assaulted by a stranger. Admitting you have a problem and talking to somebody about it is an important first step.

The Men's Advice Line offers the following advice:

⇨ Recognise that you are in an abusive relationship;
⇨ Keep a record of any incidents;
⇨ Report any incident to the police;
⇨ Seek medical attention – either from Accident & Emergency or your GP (doctor);
⇨ Take legal advice;
⇨ Don't be provoked into retaliating.

If you find yourself being physically attacked, it's important not to retaliate. Restraining somebody or hitting back leaves you liable for prosecution. If you find that you're getting into a heated argument, leave the room.

Where will I go?

Leaving your home doesn't affect your right to return, your tenancy rights or ownership of the home. Whether you rent or own your home, you have the same rights. Being assaulted by somebody you know is still a crime and you have a right to be protected under the law.

There are a handful of projects around the country that offer accommodation to male victims of domestic abuse. MALE advice line will be able to tell you if there are any in your area. Privately rented accommodation is an option, but could be expensive if you're doing it alone. Staying with your mates or family will probably be your first choice, but this may not work out over a long period of time.

19% of domestic violence incidents were reported to be male victims, with just under half of these having a female abuser

If you are homeless as a result of domestic violence, your local council housing can arrange emergency accommodation. They may ask you to provide evidence that you are being abused, which is when keeping a record of everything can be useful.

Emergency accommodation is usually in a B&B and will be for a limited period only. To apply for this you need to approach your local council housing department. Your local housing department will provide you with a list of B&Bs in the area and single male hostels.

You may decide that it is safe to return to your home if you get an injunction. There are two types:
⇨ Non-molestation Order
This is aimed at preventing your partner or ex-partner from using threatening violence against you or your children;

⇨ Occupation Order
An Occupation Order regulates who can live in the family home and can also restrict your abuser from entering the surrounding area.

Am I a victim?

Asking for help doesn't make you weak. Telling somebody that your partner is abusing you is difficult; you might feel ashamed, embarrassed or worry that you won't be taken seriously. But for all victims of domestic violence the advice is the same – you are not alone and there is help available.

Jason adds: 'I was really embarrassed but asking for help was the turning point. I realised that it does happen to other people. I left her and started re-building my life. It was hard to trust people at first, especially women, but now I'm in a loving relationship. I'll always be grateful to the people that helped me get out of my situation.'

⇨ The above information is reprinted with kind permission from TheSite.org. Visit www.thesite.org for more information.
© TheSite.org

Domestic abuse in same-sex relationships

Information from the University of Bristol

More work is needed to raise awareness of domestic abuse in same-sex relationships, according to a new study due to be discussed in Bristol next week.

The study by Professor Marianne Hester of the University of Bristol's School for Policy Studies and Dr Catherine Donovan of the University of Sunderland, reveals that most survivors of domestic abuse do not report it to organisations such as the police and domestic abuse agencies. The report says this is partly because survivors do not recognise it as domestic abuse and see it as their own problem and partly because they do not believe they will get a sympathetic response.

It concludes that training and awareness-raising about domestic abuse in same-sex relationships is needed in public agencies, particularly those in the criminal justice, domestic violence and Lesbian Gay Bisexual and Transgender fields. And they recommend that awareness-raising campaigns are conducted within LGBT communities.

The new study is the most comprehensive ever undertaken into domestic abuse in same-sex relationships in Britain and is the first in the UK to directly compare domestic abuse across same-sex and heterosexual relationships. There will be free one-day conferences in Bristol on Monday 4 December and in Newcastle on Friday 8 December to discuss the findings.

Respondents to the study indicated that, as in heterosexual relationships, a considerable number experienced domestic abuse at some time. And the report reveals that, as with heterosexual female survivors, post-separation abuse by ex-partners is a 'sizeable problem' in same-sex domestically abusive relationships.

Of those who said they had experienced domestic abuse, just over one in five (22 per cent) did not seek help from anyone. Of those who did seek help, more than half contacted friends, rather than statutory agencies. Just one in 10 contacted the police. This is in stark contrast to the much greater resort to contacting the police by all female domestic abuse victims as recorded in the British Crime Survey.

A key problem identified by the authors is that the traditional model of domestic abuse involving a male

and a female, in which the overwhelming majority of those experiencing abuse are female, hinders people in a same sex relationship from understanding that they may also be experiencing domestic abuse. They add that a lack of awareness and appropriate training among police, GPs and domestic abuse agencies in turn hinders such groups from responding in an appropriate way, although some individuals may respond sympathetically.
1 December 2006

⇨ The above information is reprinted with kind permission from the University of Bristol. Visit www. bris.ac.uk for more information.
© University of Bristol

Same-gender abuse

Fiction and facts about same-gender domestic violence

1. Fiction: Only straight women get battered; gay, bisexual, and transgendered men are never victims of domestic violence; lesbians, bisexual, and transgender women cannot batter. Battering is less common in same-gender relationships.

Fact: Men can be victims, and women can batter. Numbers reflect this: an annual study of over 2,000 gay men reflects that 1 in 4 gay men have experienced domestic violence. These numbers are consistent with research done around battering among opposite-sex couples, and lesbian couples. Stereotypes about gender and sexual orientation are repudiated by the fact that gay men are victims, and lesbians are batterers at roughly the same rate as heterosexuals are.

2. Fiction: Gay men's domestic violence is a 'fight'. Because both are men, it is a fair fight between equals.

Fact: There is nothing fair about domestic violence. This myth draws on the inability or unwillingness of many people to look at violence between two people of the same gender, particularly men, as a violent situation where one person is clearly a victim. A consensual 'fight' is not going on. A cycle of violence that includes control and domination by one of the partners is occurring. Many victims will attempt to defend themselves by fighting back. This does not make them batterers.

3. Fiction: Same-gender domestic violence is sexual behaviour, a version of sadomasochism (S & M). The victim actually likes it.

Fact: In consensual S & M, any violence, coercion, or domination occurs within the context of a mutually pleasurable 'scene', within which there is trust and/or an agreement between parties about the limits and boundaries of behaviour. In contrast, domestic violence takes place without any mutual trust or agreement, and is not consensual or pleasurable for the victim. A batterer's violent and coercive behaviours do not just affect the sexual relationship, but pervade other aspects of the relationship as well. This is not to say abuse cannot take place within S & M relationships. A batterer may actually coerce consent to violent or dominating sexual behaviour, or violate agreed-upon boundaries.

An annual study of over 2,000 gay men reflects that 1 in 4 gay men have experienced domestic violence

---

4. Fiction: Victims exaggerate the level of abuse. If it was really that bad, they would leave.

Fact: Most victims actually minimise the violence that happens to them because of the guilt, shame, and self-blame attached to victimisation, and because others do not believe them or refuse to listen. Leaving is often the hardest thing for a victim to accomplish, and is commonly harder than staying. Batterers may threaten their victims with more violence (including murder threats) if they leave. In general, incidents of domestic violence have been found to increase in severity when a victim leaves. Leaving an abusive situation requires resources such as money, housing, transportation, and support structures, all of which may have been eroded by life with an abuser.

5. Fiction: Victims provoke the violence done to them. They're 'asking for it'.

Fact: Batterers often manipulate victims to believe this myth. It perpetuates the false idea that victims are responsible for the violence done to them, that victims cause batterers to be violent. This common kind of 'victim-blaming' is powerfully destructive for survivors. In reality, whatever the situation that precedes abusive behaviour, there is always an alternative, non-violent way of responding. Batterers choose violence; victims do not 'provoke it'. Abuse is the sole responsibility of the violent person.

6. Fiction: It only happens when . . . so that's the problem, not battering.

Fact: Alcohol, drugs, work problems, jealousy, trauma histories, HIV/AIDS and stresses resulting from racism or

homophobia may all combine with battering, but they do not explain or excuse abuse. If a person who batters is also on drugs or alcohol, that person has two serious, separate problems. One does not excuse the other. Similarly, a person who has been a victim of child abuse, hate crimes, or other trauma in his or her life is not relieved of the responsibility for his or her abusive conduct.

7. Fiction: Domestic violence primarily occurs among LGBT people who hang out at bars, are poor or are people of colour.

Fact: Domestic violence is a non-discriminatory phenomenon; victims as well as violent and abusive offenders come from all walks of life, ethnic backgrounds, socioeconomic groups, and educational levels. Racist and classist stereotypes around domestic violence are common not just in the LGBT community, but also in the dominant heterosexual culture. These stereotypes are rooted in racism and classism rather than actual fact. Their perpetuation is a sign of community denial, and acts as a potential weapon for batterers who are white, educated, or of a population not generally characterised as abusive. Therapists, law enforcement officers, doctors, domestic violence workers, and

politicians are all potential batterers and victims, just like everyone else.

8. Fiction: It is easier for lesbian, gay, bisexual, or transgender victims of domestic violence to leave an abusive relationship than it is for heterosexual battered women who are married.

Fact: This myth is perpetuated by cultural homophobia which invalidates LGBT relationships as trite, false, sick, or 'just a phase'. Same-gender couples are as intertwined and involved in each other's lives as are heterosexual couples. The false assumption that LGBT people do not have children also effects the stereotype that it is easier for LGBT people to leave. Many same-gender families do have children, and many heterosexual women do not.

9. Fiction: It is not really violence when two men fight; it is normal; it is just boys being boys.

Fact: This is not true. The commonly held belief that it is acceptable and normal for men to be violent is false. There is nothing normal about domestic violence. This is much more than 'boys being boys'. It is abuse. Unfortunately, with few positive relationship role models available, many same-gender couples view and

accept violence by their partners as normal.

10. Fiction: The batterer is the bigger and stronger person; the victim is the smaller and weaker person.

Fact: This is not true. A person who is 5'7", prone to violence, and very angry can do a lot of damage to someone who is 6'2", twenty pounds heavier, and a non-violent person. Size, weight, butchness, queeniness, or any other physical attribute or role are not good indicators of whether or not a man will be a victim or a batterer. This myth focuses only on the physical aspects of domestic violence. A batterer does not need to be built like a linebacker to smash your compact discs, cut up all your clothing, or threaten to tell everyone at work that you are really a queer. Violence is a matter of personal choice, not body size.

⇨ Adapted from material in *Men Who Beat The Men Who Love Them*, by David Island and Patrick Letellier, material from the Violence Recovery Program at FCHC, and Wingspan Domestic Violence Project. This information appears on the website of the Metropolitan Police Service and is reprinted with their permission.

Spyware: another weapon for domestic abuse

Remote controlling spouses

Spyware is becoming a tool of domestic abuse, according to security researchers.

Privacy-invading software packages are most commonly associated with surreptitiously snooping on victims to find out the passwords they use for online banking sites or bombarding them with invasive pop-up ads. But spyware can also be used as a tool to monitor and control their spouses by abusive partners, McAfee researcher Anna Stepanov warns.

By John Leyden

'With so much of our lives dependent on computers and other technologies such as cell phones, the use of spyware is ideal for abusers, who often feel the need to control all aspects of a victim's existence,' she writes. 'Monitoring a victim's online, cell phone, or general computing activity is of more value than ever in controlling or hurting a victim.'

Safe computing has joined finding safe housing as a list of requirements for people fleeing abusive relationships. 'There is a strong movement within the [US-based] National Network to End Domestic Violence to educate victims and the general public about safe computing,' Stepanov adds. 'Many security companies have made sizable monetary donations to this organisation to assist in education and to provide aid for securing networks within shelters for victims of domestic violence.'

The changing uses of spyware and its continuing evolution are dealt with in a white paper by Stepanov titled *Spyware: A Morphing Campaign.*

Commercial products such as FlexiSPY, which records information about an individual's mobile phone calls and SMS messages before sending them to a remote server, have already generated controversy over the last couple of years. Packages such as FlexiSPY and Mobile Spy, another similar product, are marketed as a means for parents to keep watch on their child's phone, or enable employers to enforce an acceptable use policy on their staff. The legality of both products has been questioned.

A mobile phone is an obvious target for snoopers, but email inboxes are also a tempting target for control-freaks looking to keep tabs on their partners. Stepanov's research shows that cybercrime in its traditional sense is not the only motive for planting spyware.

31 January 2008

⇨ The above information is reprinted with kind permission from The Register. Visit www.theregister.co.uk for more information.

© *The Register*

Forced marriage

Extract from a report by Manchester City Council. By Sarah Khalil

Narina's story

'I felt that I had no option. Once they had taken me out of the country there was nothing I could do. I had no contact with anyone but the family. My mother was caught between my feelings and the community's expectations. They made me feel that I would dishonour my family if I didn't marry him.'

Narina was 18 when her parents took her back home for a family holiday. She was kept in the family home and wasn't allowed out on her own. Finally she and her sister managed to run away and contacted the British Consulate, who found her a place to stay and helped her contact her friends in the UK. She eventually came home and with the help of a women's refuge and her friends, has built a new life for herself and her sister.

Taken from 'What is forced marriage' leaflet published by the Foreign and Commonwealth office (FCO).

Introduction

The definition of domestic abuse includes forced marriage. The Manchester Crime and Disorder Reduction Partnership defines domestic abuse as 'any incident of threatening behaviour, violence or abuse (psychological, physical, sexual, financial or emotional) between adults who are or have been, intimate partners of family members, regardless of gender or sexuality'. Forced marriage is different to an arranged marriage in that if a marriage is forced one or both parties do not consent to the marriage and some element of duress is involved.

Duress can include both physical and emotional abuse.

Parents who force their children to marry often justify their behaviour as protecting their children, building stronger families and preserving cultural or religious traditions. They often do not see anything wrong in their actions. Forced marriage cannot be justified on religious grounds: every major faith condemns it and freely given consent is a prerequisite of Christian, Jewish, Hindu, Muslim and Sikh marriages.

The definition of domestic abuse includes forced marriage

Most victims are in their early teens to late twenties. In some instances, an agreement may have been made about marriage when a child is in their infancy. Manchester Safeguarding Board understands forced marriage to be a form of abuse. Forced marriage, has existed for centuries in many cultures. It is not just a South Asian/Muslim problem but affects other faiths and ethnic groups. It is a global issue and a violation of human rights.

Although men can be affected, evidence shows that cases overwhelmingly involve young women and girls. Women experience greater pressures in greater numbers. In certain communities women marry at a younger age than men and are less likely to have the chance to complete their education or establish a professional career.

In addition, such women have less choice over their overall lifestyles, such as the ability to go out and mix with friends, even female friends. Women have less choice over marriage partners and pre-marital relationships are often prohibited.

Women encountering forced marriage are placed under considerable pressure to stay in or reconcile themselves to abusive situations and face severe consequences for having shamed their family: social ostracism, harassment and other acts of violence, including 'honour' killings/murders. Often this choice of whether to accept the abuse of forced marriage or lose the family they need and love is a very difficult decision for a young person in particular. Those who lose their family but escape the forced marriage often still go on to experience depression and anxiety as they grieve the loss of their family.

Men forced into marriage can be abusive to their spouse and are more likely to commit adultery, and domestic abuse such as neglect, abandonment and marital rape.

Frequently, when an initial referral is made to a statutory or voluntary sector agency such as Children's Social Care, Police or Women's Aid, the person may not mention the words forced marriage. Cases may present with a variety of problems such as truancy, a person reported missing or episodes of depression or self-harm. Professionals need to be sensitive to the fact that these presenting problems could mean that forced marriage is an underlying issue, and ensure that they consider this when dealing with the case.

Figures and statistics

In many cases people experiencing forced marriage may present with issues including domestic abuse, child abuse, homelessness or health problems. Data around these problems is gathered by various agencies but the underlying problem of forced marriage may not be identified.

Data that we are aware of shows that each year the Forced Marriage Unit (FMU) receives approximately 5,000 calls from professionals and victims. Of these 300 turn into actual cases. Approximately 35% of cases referred to the Unit are from the North West of England. 30% of cases involve minors (some as young as 8 years of age) and 15% involve men. The FMU generally assists British people being forced or who have been forced into marriage. Their data does not therefore reflect the number of non-British citizens forced into marriage abroad who are brought over to the UK.

The data does not show the whole picture. We know that in 2006/07 the Manchester Domestic Abuse Helpline received 65 calls out of 7,758 in relation to forced marriage and Central Manchester Women's Aid assisted 40 women affected by forced marriage out of a total client group of 95 in a one-year period. Nationally Women's Aid recorded 194 calls were forced marriage out of 3,051 callers whom they asked during 2006/07.

Over the years organisations such as Southall Black Sisters and Saheli Women's Refuge as part of Manchester Women's Aid, South Manchester Law Centre, Asian Youth Movement in the 80s and 90s have campaigned on this issue including supporting victims and survivors of forced marriage.

In 1999 the Home Office established a working group to investigate the extent of the problem of forced marriage. It published a report in June 2000, *A Choice by Right*. Following that report, the government produced guidelines for the police, social services, education and health. Manchester has forced marriage protocols for both adults and for children and

young people. The adults' protocol is currently being reviewed and updated by the Accommodation and Support Subgroup of the Domestic Abuse Management Group (DAMG). Forced marriage training is available for professionals in Manchester. This ensures that best practice is followed by providing professionals with guidance and the contact details of domestic abuse agencies and the FMU. Recently Manchester's Domestic Abuse Coordinator and the Adult Protection Coordinator provided comment on the Foreign and Commonwealth Office's latest guidelines for working with vulnerable adults affected by forced marriage.

Research

Recently Central Manchester Women's Aid were involved in Home Office research covering Manchester and London. The research, which is awaiting validation, looked into whether or not increasing the legal age of marriage to 21 or 25 years of age before a spouse visa can be granted would decrease the incidence of forced marriage. The findings concluded that this would not help as young people could be taken abroad at 16 or 18 years of age for example then forced to stay there until they were old enough to return with their spouse. This could therefore increase the period of abuse that they experience.

The research made several recommendations including to work in more inclusive ways so not only focusing on South Asian women but other communities as well. Manchester's domestic abuse agencies are currently working within local communities to ensure that services are available to all groups. This work is lead by the Communications Subgroup of the DAMG. Another recommendation of the research was for more preventative work to be done in schools. In November 2007 Manchester Domestic Abuse Management Group will be launching the Domestic Abuse Education Pack in schools which has a range of PSHE materials within it covering the issue of forced marriage as a part of domestic abuse.

Legal powers

Although there is no specific criminal

offence of 'forcing someone to marry' within England and Wales, criminal offences may nevertheless be committed. Perpetrators – usually parents or family members – could be prosecuted for offences including threatening behaviour, assault, kidnap, abduction, rape, threats to kill, imprisonment and murder. The existing legal framework affords a great deal of protection to children and young people at risk of being forced into marriage. The Manchester Safeguarding Children Board supports agencies in ensuring that the powers are proactively applied, and promotes the training of individuals and agencies to respond positively to referral and identification of forced marriage.

The new 2007 Forced Marriage (Civil Protection) Act will assist in protecting individuals from being forced or who have been forced to enter into marriage. This Act allows legal protection orders to be made and has served the valuable purpose of raising the issue in an educative way amongst the judiciary.

Conclusion

When an adult is forced into marriage they are also experiencing domestic abuse. If a child is forced into marriage they are subjected to child abuse. The Domestic Abuse Management Group in partnership with the Manchester Safeguarding Children Board are working on a variety of initiatives to support victims, hold perpetrators accountable and protect children and young people.

Manchester is working hard to tackle domestic and child abuse. Progress is being made through for example our dedicated court, sanctuary schemes which provide extra security in a victim's home and our Multi Agency Risk Assessment Conferences which target support to the most high risk victims of domestic abuse. Our partnership approach with specialist workers and the FMU ensures a coordinated community response to forced marriage and domestic abuse.
16 October 2007

⇨ Information from Manchester City Council. Visit www.manchester.gov.uk for more.

Zena's story

Information from The Hideout

In my community the idea of privacy really doesn't exist. Everyone knows everything about each other. Sometimes it feels like you have about 20 sets of parents. Everyone else always seems to know what's best for you and where your life is going.

My dad was the one who brought my mum over to the UK when they got married. Their parents had arranged the marriage. My mum said she learned to love my dad over the years and she was really happy to live in England. But she didn't like that my dad wouldn't let her work. My dad is really traditional and always says he thinks it's terrible how English girls don't respect their families. I can't remember a time when mum and dad weren't fighting about something.

I love both my mum and dad but sometimes I feel lost because the traditions we have at home are so different from everything around me. Last year I cut my hair short because I wanted to be more like the other girls in my school; my dad got really cross and wouldn't let me leave the house for three months, except to go to school.

All that my dad ever talks about is the boy I'm going to marry. This boy doesn't live here and I've never met him. I don't want to marry him – I get scared thinking about it. Every year my dad talks more and more about this boy I will marry soon.

My dad says that next summer we're going on holiday to his country. Since he said that, the fighting between my mum and him has been really horrible. Almost every day when I get home from school there's a row. I just go to my room and close the door, but I'm really afraid. I think their fights are about my mum asking my dad not to take my sister and me to be married. Sometimes I hear my dad hitting my mum, but my mum never talks about it.

Forcing someone into marriage is against a person's rights. It can also be part of domestic violence

---

My dad is never in a happy mood any more and shouts at me nearly every day. He threatens to lock me in the house and not let me see any of my friends. He says he'll hurt me if I don't marry the boy he's chosen; he says I'll shame our whole family if I don't. I can't concentrate in school and I don't feel happy any more. Things got so bad at home that I wanted to leave. But I didn't know where I could go and I worried too much about what would happen to my mum and my sister if I ran away.

I talked to a friend at school whose parents also believe in arranging marriages and not in 'love' marriages. She said that her parents also want to force her into a marriage. She told me she used to hurt herself to try to numb the pain. It felt so good to hear that I wasn't the only one feeling so unhappy! My friend said that ever since she spoke to her learning mentor at school, she's felt better. Her learning mentor suggested that she also speak to a local group who can help girls like us.

We decided to go to that group together. At least I don't feel so alone any more. I've learned about my rights. Forcing someone into marriage is against a person's rights. It can also be part of domestic violence. The people who work there told us that it happens to a lot of other girls and boys as well. They talk to me about what choices I have and that if the abuse gets worse at home, I can go to a refuge. They understand that I don't really want to leave my family because I love them. They're helping me talk to my dad's sister and brother. Hopefully they can change his mind.

I don't want to bring shame on my family, but I know I want to make my own decisions in life. I want to be a doctor, so I'm working really hard in school and one day I hope to marry someone I fall in love with and who treats me well. Things are still difficult at home and I'm not sure how they'll turn out, but I feel like I can talk to people who understand and hopefully they'll be able to help.

⇨ The above information is re-printed with kind permission from The Hideout. Visit www.thehideout.org.uk for more information.

© Women's Aid

Impact of domestic violence on children

Some of the biggest victims of domestic violence are the smallest. New global report from UNICEF reveals impact of domestic violence on children

A global study published today by UNICEF and The Body Shop International reveals the devastating and lasting impact on children of living with domestic violence.

Defining domestic violence as the physical, sexual or mental abuse of a parent or caregiver, the report finds that the experience of watching, hearing or otherwise being aware of domestic violence can impact children's physical, emotional and social development, both during childhood and later in life.

In the vast majority of cases, domestic violence is perpetrated against women. At least one in three women globally has been beaten, coerced into sex, or abused in some other way – most often by someone she knows, including by her husband or another male family member. Globally, one woman in four has been abused during pregnancy. The report turns attention to the lesser-known facts: the impact on children who are exposed to this violence.

Based on global data from the United Nations Secretary-General's Study on Violence against Children, the report conservatively estimates that as many as 275 million children are currently exposed to domestic violence. The fact that domestic violence is chronically under-reported and that some countries have no data at all makes it difficult to quantify how many children it affects.

'Domestic violence can have a lasting negative impact on children,' UNICEF Executive Director Ann M. Veneman said in New York. 'It is critical that children grow up in safe and stable environments, free of violence.'

The Body Shop International is helping to take action against domestic violence by launching its 2006 Stop Violence in the Home Campaign, which focuses on children as the forgotten victims.

Dame Anita Roddick, Founder of The Body Shop, added, 'Our report shows that some of the biggest victims of domestic violence are the smallest. Protecting children should be the absolute concern of everybody who is working to see an end to domestic violence. We urge everyone to rally behind this global campaign.'

The lasting impact of domestic violence on children

The report finds that children who live with domestic violence not only endure the distress of being surrounded by violence, but are more likely to become victims of abuse themselves. An estimated 40 per cent of child-abuse victims also have reported domestic violence in the home.

Even when children are not physically abused themselves, their exposure to domestic violence can have severe and lasting effects. The impact begins early: studies show that younger children are more likely to be exposed to domestic violence than older children, which can impair their mental and emotional growth in a critical stage of development.

As they grow up, children who are exposed to domestic violence continue to face a range of possible effects including trouble with school work, limited social skills, depression, anxiety and other psychological problems. They are at greater risk for substance abuse, teenage pregnancy and delinquent behaviour, according to the report.

The report also finds that the single best predictor of children continuing the cycle of domestic violence – either as perpetrators or as victims – depends on whether or not they grow up in a home with domestic violence. Research shows that rates of abuse are higher among women whose husbands were abused as children or who saw their mothers being abused. Many studies have also found that children from violent homes show signs of more aggressive behaviour, such as bullying, and are up to three times more likely to be involved in fighting.

The report urges governments and societies to pay more attention to the specific needs of children who live in homes impacted by domestic violence. It also identifies the need for better monitoring and reporting on the prevalence of domestic violence in order to shed light on this hidden issue.

Governments have a vital role to play in breaking the cycle of domestic violence and protecting the youngest victims of domestic violence, and are urged to:

⇨ Raise awareness of the impact of domestic violence on children through public education campaigns and efforts to challenge beliefs and customs that condone violence.

⇨ Create public policies and laws that protect children. Governments must enact and enforce laws and policies that criminalise domestic violence and protect all its victims.

⇨ Improve social services that address the impact of violence in the home on children. Interventions that support children who are exposed to domestic violence help minimise the long-term risks to these children and must be adequately funded and scaled up.

The Body Shop's Stop Violence in the Home campaign aims to raise awareness and to encourage governments to better protect and support children who are exposed to domestic violence.

1 August 2006

⇨ The above information is reprinted with kind permission from UNICEF. Visit www.unicef.org for more information.

© UNICEF

Children and domestic violence

Information from End the Fear

Children are individuals and can be affected by domestic violence in lots of different ways. However, the one thing we can all be sure about is that the violence is almost certainly having an impact on them in the short and the longer term.

All children will be aware on a daily basis of the unpredictability of the situation in which they live, the tension, and the fear and intimidation, which means that the man is able to rule and terrorise everyone in their home.

Many children will be shocked, embarrassed, and blame themselves for the violence (as their mothers do also) and will look desperately for solutions within themselves to end the violence. Many children (especially older children) will fantasise about hurting, or killing the man, as a way of stopping the violence.

The effects on children tend to vary according to how old they are and also according to the levels of violence, the length of time the violence has been happening for and how much support they've had from others around them. If you are an abused women it is important to know the most common ways in which your child/ren may be impacted.

Under-2s

⇨ Be easily frightened and/or nervous.

⇨ Be frightened of your partner and possibly of men in general.

⇨ Be very demanding.

⇨ Cry a lot.

⇨ Have broken sleep or nightmares.

⇨ Be very clingy towards you and not cope well with being separated.

⇨ Be very clingy towards your partner.

⇨ Have an unusual amount of temper tantrums.

⇨ Not eat well and be underweight.

⇨ Have slow speech development and/or coordination skills.

⇨ Be slow to learn to crawl and/or walk.

⇨ Stop doing things they have already learnt and return to more babyish behaviour (e.g. stopping walking).

⇨ Be aggressive towards you and/or other children.

2 to 5-year-olds

⇨ Be easily frightened and/or nervous.

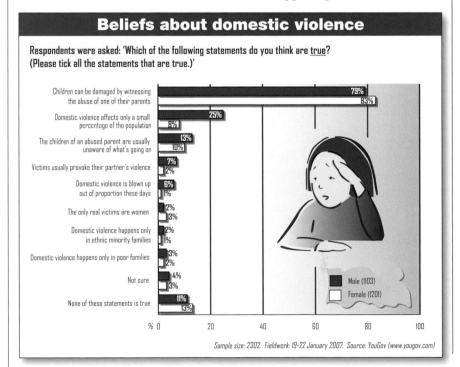

Beliefs about domestic violence

Respondents were asked: 'Which of the following statements do you think are true? (Please tick all the statements that are true.)'

Statement	Male (1103)	Female (1201)
Children can be damaged by witnessing the abuse of one of their parents	79%	83%
Domestic violence affects only a small percentage of the population	25%	8%
The children of an abused parent are usually unaware of what's going on	13%	10%
Victims usually provoke their partner's violence	7%	2%
Domestic violence is blown up out of proportion these days	6%	1%
The only real victims are women	2%	3%
Domestic violence happens only in ethnic minority families	2%	1%
Domestic violence happens only in poor families	3%	2%
Not sure	4%	3%
None of these statements is true	11%	13%

Sample size: 2302. Fieldwork: 19-22 January 2007. Source: YouGov (www.yougov.com)

⇨ Be frightened of your partner and possibly of men in general.

⇨ Be very clingy towards you and/or your partner and not cope well with being separated.

⇨ Have an unusual amount of temper tantrums.

⇨ Cry a lot.

⇨ Not show much emotion (either happy or sad) and may seem detached.

⇨ Be aggressive towards you and/or other children.

⇨ Try to stop the violence and may feel guilty when they can't succeed in this.

⇨ Try to hurt themselves.

⇨ Have slow development or regress (e.g. wet themselves or the bed after being toilet trained).

5 to 11-year-olds

⇨ Be easily frightened, nervous or worried.

⇨ Be very demanding.

⇨ Actively try to stop the violence (possibly getting hurt in the process).

⇨ Behave well at home but be very aggressive and/or rude to others at school.

⇨ May be looking after you or their siblings.

⇨ Bully other children at school and/or brothers and sisters.

⇨ Not like themselves as they think that the violence is their fault.

⇨ Be angry with your partner.

⇨ Be angry with you and may blame you for the violence.

⇨ Sometimes it feels safer for children to express their anger towards the non-violent parent than the violent parent, or the violent partner will tell the child it's the non-violent parent's fault.

⇨ May try to please your violent partner and/or copy some of his behaviour.

⇨ Do badly or very well at school. Some children find it difficult to concentrate on schoolwork because they're worrying about what's happening at home. Others try to block out their home life by only focusing on their schoolwork. Many people wrongly assume that children doing very well at school have not been affected.

All children will be aware on a daily basis of the unpredictability of the situation in which they live, the tension, and the fear and intimidation

---

⇨ Constantly complain of feeling ill to avoid going to school when the doctor can't find anything wrong (child may be worried about what will happen to mum while they're at school).

⇨ Find it difficult to make friends at school (sometimes because the child feels too 'different' from others and can't relate to them and sometimes because they miss out on having friends come home due to their fear of what might happen there).

⇨ Take on responsibilities inappropriate to their age (e.g. childcare or household tasks).

⇨ Be depressed.

11 to 17-year-olds

⇨ Be very demanding.

⇨ Fight a lot with friends and/or brothers and sisters.

⇨ May have to look after you or parent their siblings.

⇨ Not get on well at school or do unusually well by focusing exclusively on schoolwork instead of on social or family life.

⇨ Behave very badly at school in the hope of getting the attention of the school.

⇨ May truant from school.

⇨ Be depressed and/or anxious and/or fearful.

⇨ Be confused about the roles of men and women (boys may be afraid of growing up for fear of becoming like their dads).

⇨ Run away from home.

⇨ Try to protect their mum from the violence and may be hurt in this process.

⇨ Be abusive towards their mum (copying dad's behaviour).

⇨ Turn to drugs or alcohol to try to escape from reality. (For help and advice on drugs and alcohol abuse please contact the CAT team or the Drugs Team.)

If you think that your child is affected by the violence then it's important to talk to them and try to offer your support. You can also get additional help from a number of organisations.

⇨ The above information is reprinted with kind permission from End the Fear. Visit www.endthefear.co.uk for more information.

© End the Fear

'I loved and hated my father then; I love and hate him still'

Clare Barnes grew up watching her father beat her mother. As a child she felt torn – whose side should she be on? Now that her parents are old, and the violence continues, so too does her confusion

On Saturday morning my mother left with £250 in her purse. It was every penny she had saved for months for our Christmas toys and food. She returned in the early evening. In her single shopping bag was a frying pan. She had £1 left in her purse. She could not explain where the rest of the money had gone. My father beat her senseless.

First he slapped her in the face, forcing her head to swing violently, as if her neck was made from string. 'What did you do with my money?' he screeched, the spit spraying from his mouth. She looked at him through glassy eyes, bewildered, drunk and incapable of concealing the fact.

He kicked her up and down our dingy little living room, his face crimson with fury. I watched through my fingers from the corner, begging him to stop. I was eight years old.

A couple of years later, when my mother was seven months pregnant with my younger brother, she arrived home from another seasonal shopping excursion. This time she had bags of goodies. As soon as she opened her mouth I knew she was drunk. I also knew I had to do something. My father would be back in half an hour.

I made her a cup of tea, sat her down in front of the TV, woke her up when she appeared to be nodding off. Then he came home. At first, at the sight of the shopping bags, it seemed as if he might overlook her condition. Then he realised no supper had been prepared.

A beating ensued of such relentless barbarity that the next day her face was so bruised I didn't recognise her. I told Anne, my six-year-old sister, that our mother was ill and was not to be disturbed. Anne diligently avoided my parents' bedroom.

Brian was born a few days after Christmas, five weeks premature and weighing just a few pounds. We all knew, but never said out loud, that the beatings were partly to blame.

One in four women in the UK will experience domestic violence at least once in their lives, according to the charity Women's Aid, and tens of thousands of children will witness or be a victim of it

---

To those who have never experienced domestic violence or witnessed it, it can be a complete mystery why women stay with men who abuse them, or why the children of families where domestic violence occurs don't respond to it in the same way.

One in four women in the UK will experience domestic violence at least once in their lives, according to the charity Women's Aid, and tens of thousands of children will witness or be a victim of it. Research shows that women (it is almost always women who are the victims) stay in these destructive relationships for all kinds of reasons including financial necessity and a fear of worse violence if they leave.

Through the eyes of children, the boundaries between victim and perpetrator are not always clear cut. Studies conducted by a number of the charities that support victims show that children can be ambivalent. Often, as coping mechanisms, they take sides, or they go about trying to defuse the violence. Some children pretend it isn't happening, while others blame themselves for not being able to stop it.

My older sister, Ellen, became detached. Despite being three years older than me, she seemed content to leave me in charge of calming the storms. She placed the blame firmly on my mother. 'If she didn't drink, he wouldn't hit her,' Ellen told me once when I tried to explain that our mother had problems that made her drink. One day when I came home from school I found Ellen sitting on the sofa, motionless, watching as our father pummelled our mother. It was as if she was watching something on television.

Anne, on the other hand, was needy and she looked to me for comfort. I became a parent-figure to both her and Brian, who, from the moment he could speak, seemed like a fragile little soul.

Though still a child, I instinctively tried to protect my younger siblings. I believed it was my duty. I don't know

why. Sometimes, during the beatings, I would shuffle Anne and Brian into a bedroom and turn the radio up loud to drown out the noise. I would play games with them to focus their minds on something else. If they were adequately distracted, I would venture downstairs to negotiate a truce. Later, when alone in bed, I would allow myself to cry.

My father chose to deal with my mother's erratic behaviour (which was fuelled by an alcohol problem and addiction to prescription anti-depressants) with his fists. Alcohol is frequently given as a reason for domestic violence but my father rarely drank. Drunk or sober, the mere sight of my mother intoxicated was enough to trigger a frenzied assault.

Between incidents, my father and my mother were openly affectionate and enjoyed a similar sense of humour. But in many ways, these intervals of 'normality' were part of the problem. We could never totally relax. Even if we went months without an incident, the next one hung over us like an impending hurricane. We knew it was coming and that it would leave destruction in its wake. The only question was how much.

I loved and hated my father then; I love and hate him still. It is a difficult thing to reconcile and even harder to explain to other people. He was a monster, but he was also a popular, playful, warm man. I have many fond memories of him during my childhood.

I would never excuse my father's behaviour but, unlike many perpetrators of domestic violence, he never once raised a hand to any of his children, and I am grateful to him for this. I never felt threatened by him – even during the most ferocious outbursts. But to this day, it breaks my heart that he never seemed to register that by attacking our mother he was abusing us too.

Documentary evidence from women who have been abused in their homes shows that many violent men apologise profusely and beg forgiveness after incidents. The women who take them back often do so because of the their professed contrition and their apparently sincere pledges that this time was the last time. In the case of my father, he would often sit on the sofa weeping like a little boy. He sometimes held me close to him, telling me how sorry he was and that I had to understand that she angered him so much he couldn't help himself.

The thing is, at the time I could see it from his point of view. My mother was mentally ill and her problems put all of us under enormous pressure. There were other factors too. We were always struggling to make ends meet, and he was often out of work. I comforted him because, like my mother in her more lucid moments, I really wanted to believe that maybe, just maybe, this was the last time it would happen.

While a teenager, I came to realise that my family's experiences were not unique. It helped. There were at least three homes in our street where domestic violence was a regular occurrence. When I was 11, I witnessed the father of my closest friend hold a carving knife to the throat of his wife as she lay cowering on the sofa. I remember thinking, with relief, that at least my father had never used a weapon. Everything is relative. My friend – as she always did under such circumstances – became hysterical. When her father heard her screams, he turned and threatened her with the knife. As was the case for my family, the police were never called and no charges were ever pressed. The time when the police treated domestic violence as a 'family issue' and not a criminal one is gone, but, according to Victim Support, the number of women who do not press charges remains shockingly high.

My father continues to beat my mother (although as he has aged he seems to have lost his appetite for it, so the incidents are fewer and less brutal). I still wonder what I should do about it. Do I have him, a 65-year-old man with health problems, arrested? Do I persist in trying to persuade her to leave him? It is an anguished decision, yet my answer to both questions is no.

As Christmas approaches, my thoughts, as they have done every year since I left home, turn to this issue. For most of the year it is something relegated to the back of my mind, but something about the smug family images that herald the approach of 25 December propel me backwards. I always come back to the same question: what effect did all those years of violence have on our family? The passing of time does not make it any easier to answer. My brother has beaten his wife on occasion. Would he have done it even if he hadn't witnessed it himself? Who knows? Have my sisters been beaten? I don't know. Would they tell me if they had, or, as is still the case for many victims, would they be too ashamed to admit it, even to close relatives?

As for me, over the years I have reacted in many ways (and probably some I can't identify). When I was a teenager living at home, I swung with alarming regularity from one extreme to another: from a desperate need to stay calm and look after those around me, to being consumed with so much rage I contemplated knocking my father out with the nearest blunt instrument.

At times I sat curled in a ball in the corner of my bedroom listening helplessly to muffled arguments reach an inevitable nadir with the sound of my mother's body thumping against a wall and her whimpering cries for mercy. I spent a lot of time day-dreaming. The most comforting dream was my favourite teacher asking me to live with her.

When I turned 13, I went wild for a while, getting drunk with my friends. I still carry the guilt of having left Anne and Brian to fend for themselves. I'm not sure when exactly, or what triggered it, but I decided that I had to get out. I knuckled down at school and made it my mission to get to university. I applied to one hundreds of miles away. I realised that if I was to stand any chance of happiness in life, I would have to be as far away as possible.

By my 20s, no matter how much geography I had put between me and my past, I never felt truly extricated. For years I was irrationally close to believing that all men are potential abusers. After all, if my father, an otherwise likable, loving man, could do it, couldn't anyone? I have mellowed with age (possibly on the back of relationships where I have been treated with nothing but respect).

But even now, if someone raises their voice around me, I bristle with dread and am momentarily catapulted back to being eight years old.

In the run-up to Christmas there is always a sinister sense of portent that I can never quite shake off. A few years ago, when I saw the film *East is East* (which contains a poignantly resonant scene of domestic violence) I left the cinema and sobbed convulsively for three hours. I wept for my mother, for myself, and for my brother and sisters. I wept for all the families where women were being beaten at that moment and would be beaten in the future. And I wept for my father.

⇨ Clare Barnes is a pseudonym.

9 December 2006

Domestic violence statistics

Key child protection statistics (December 2007)

⇨ 29% of women and 18% of men aged 16 to 59 reported that they had experienced one or more types of abuse (non-sexual abuse such as use of physical force, being prevented from having money or seeing friends or being belittled, sexual assault and stalking) at the hands of a current or former partner at some time since age 16.

Coleman, K. et al. (2007) Homicides, firearm offences and intimate violence 2005/2006: supplementary volume 1 to Crime in England and Wales 2005/2006 (PDF). London: Home Office. Research, Development and Statistics Directorate.

⇨ One in five women (19%) and one in ten men (10%) reported that they had experienced physical force by a partner or former partner at some time since age 16.

Coleman, K. et al. (2007) Homicides, firearm offences and intimate violence 2005/2006: supplementary volume 1 to Crime in England and Wales 2005/2006 (PDF). London: Home Office. Research, Development and Statistics Directorate.

⇨ Domestic violence accounts for 15% of all violent crime.

Walker, A. et al. (2006) Crime in England and Wales 2005/2006 (PDF). London: Home Office. Research, Development and Statistics Directorate.

⇨ Over a quarter (26%) of young adults reported that physical violence sometimes took place between those caring for them during childhood. For 5% this violence was constant or frequent.

Cawson, P. (2002) Child maltreatment in the family. London: NSPCC. p.37.

⇨ There is 'a strong overlap between physical, sexual and emotional abuse of children and domestic violence, and high proportions of those experiencing abuse from parents also experienced frequent violence between carers. The findings demonstrate the importance of identifying and addressing domestic violence as a predictor of child maltreatment.'

Cawson, P. (2002) Child maltreatment in the family: the experience of a national sample of young people. London: NSPCC. p.78.

⇨ There is a strong correlation between domestic violence and child maltreatment:

↳ for those young adults who said that during childhood they had been neglected, 88% had lived with some level of domestic violence, and for 59% the violence was constant or frequent.

↳ for those young adults who said that during childhood they had been physically abused, 75% had lived with some level of domestic violence, and for 36% the violence was constant or frequent.

- for those young adults who said that during childhood they had been emotionally abused, 71% had lived with some level of domestic violence, and for 48% the violence was constant or frequent.
- for those young adults who said that during childhood they had been sexually abused, 54% had lived with some level of domestic violence, and for 20% the violence was constant or frequent.

The total cost of domestic violence to services amounts to £3.1 billion per year

Cawson, P. (2002) Child mal-treatment in the family: the experience of a national sample of young people. London: NSPCC. p.37-38.

⇨ Between 1994 and 2004, 29 children in 13 families were killed during contact (or in one case residence) arrangements in England and Wales. Ten of these children were killed in the last two years.
Saunders, H. (2004) 29 child homicides: lessons still to be learnt on domestic violence and child protection. [Bristol]: Women's Aid Federation of England (WAFE).

⇨ The total cost of domestic violence to services (the criminal justice system, health, social services, housing and civil legal) amounts to £3.1 billion per year, while the loss to the economy is £2.7 billion per year in England and Wales. 'An additional element is the human and emotional cost. Domestic violence leads to pain and suffering that is not counted in the cost of services. This amounts to over £17 billion a year. Including all costs, the total cost of domestic violence for the state, employers and victims is estimated at around £23 billion [per year].'
Walby, S. (2004) The cost of domestic violence (PDF). London: DTI, Women and Equality Unit.

Domestic violence – calls to ChildLine 2005/2006

⇨ 289 children calling ChildLine in 2005/2006 gave domestic violence as their main problem (of which 230 were girls and 59 were boys – i.e. 4 girls to every 1 boy). 1,432 children gave domestic violence as an additional problem in 2005/2006 (of which 1,151 were girls and 281 were boys). Therefore in 2005/2006, a total of 1,721 children calling ChildLine spoke about domestic violence in their call. This was 1% of all callers.

Domestic violence accounts for 15% of all violent crime

⇨ 39% of children counselled by ChildLine about domestic violence in 2005/2006 went on to talk about family relationship problems. 15% went on to talk about being physically abused themselves, and 10% talked about emotional abuse. A further 10% went on to talk about feeling at risk of abuse themselves. 27% of children counselled about domestic violence did not go on to talk about any other problem.

⇨ The ages of children calling ChildLine where domestic violence was given as a main problem during 2005/2006 were as follows:[1]
- age unknown: 16% (46);
- 5-11 years: 26% (64);
- 12-15 years: 44% (107);
- 16-18 years: 30% (72).

⇨ No referrals were made about children who had called ChildLine about domestic violence during 2005/2006.
ChildLine data (2005/2006) – unpublished.

Footnote

1. Percentages apply to those records where this information was given.
December 2007

⇨ Information from the NSPCC. Visit www.nspcc.org.uk for more.
© NSPCC

Male and female views of domestic violence

Respondents were asked: 'What is your view of men who say they have been victims of domestic violence? (Please tick the statement that comes closest to your view.)'

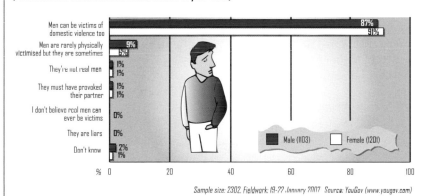

Sample size: 2302. Fieldwork: 19-22 January 2007. Source: YouGov (www.yougov.com)

Respondents were asked: 'Which, if any, of these do you regard as domestic violence? (Please tick all to which you think the term applies.)'

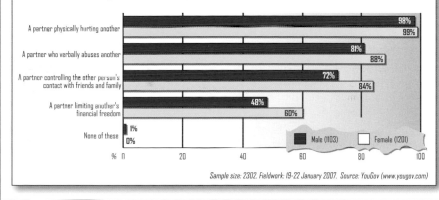

Sample size: 2302. Fieldwork: 19-22 January 2007. Source: YouGov (www.yougov.com)

Gender violence among teenagers

42% of young people know girls whose boyfriends have hit them – new survey

A new ICM survey commissioned by the End Violence Against Women campaign (EVAW) has found that 42% of young people know girls whose boyfriends have hit them and that 40% know girls whose boyfriends have coerced or pressurised them to have sex (1).

The survey, carried out amongst people aged 16-20 across the UK, also found that 59% of young people feel they do not have enough information and support to advise those they know who may have been the victims of physical or sexual violence.

The EVAW campaign is calling for the survey to act as a prompt for greater action from the Government in combating violence against women, including providing far more support and resources for young people in schools, clubs, colleges and workplaces.

Over two-thirds (68%) of female respondents to the survey said that they lacked support and information for dealing with violence against women, while more than half of males (51%) said the same thing.

The Government's own recently launched Action Plan on Social Exclusion noted poor knowledge and skills among young people in relation to sex, relationships and sexual health risks, leading to a lack of confidence to resist pressure to engage in early sexual activity. However, Personal Social and Health Education (PSHE) continues to be a non-statutory subject and violence against women is not even identified in the existing guidelines.

The End Violence Against Women Campaign Chair Liz Kelly said:

'It's distressing that violence against women is not only widespread, but in young people's lives so directly, and that a majority of 16-20-year-olds admit they are unsure what advice to give girls they know who have been assaulted.

'We're calling for a major effort from the Government to combat endemic levels of violence against girls and women in this country.

'If the Government is serious about preventing violence against women, as well as providing quality support services, it must ensure that young people have the opportunity to discuss it at school – learning about these issues is as much a part of young people's educational entitlement as learning to read.'

A significant minority of young people held views that condoned sexual violence

The survey had other surprising results regarding young people's attitudes towards violence against women. While an overwhelming majority of respondents recognised that physical violence against a partner is unacceptable (more than 95%), a significant minority of young people held views that condoned sexual violence.

For example, 27% thought it was acceptable for a boy to 'expect to have sex with a girl' if the girl has been 'very flirtatious'. The same view was held by one in twelve (8%) of young people in the case of situations where a boy had 'spent a lot of time and money' on the girl. Eleven per cent thought it was acceptable for a boy to expect to have sex if sexual activity had been initiated and the boy was 'really turned on'. In most cases more young men held these views than young women.

These views reflect those revealed in a 2005 ICM poll of British adults that found that around a third of people believed that in some circumstances, such as having been flirtatious or being drunk, a woman could be held responsible for being raped (2).

Liz Kelly added:

'The survey shows that in addition to being exposed to violence against women, a sizeable minority of young people harbour attitudes that condone it, especially coercive sex.

'Attitudes that underpin gender violence need to be challenged at the same time as doing more to actually safeguard girls and women.'

The survey comes ahead of a new EVAW report on the Government's record in combating violence against women due to be published on Thursday (23 November).

This report, 'Making the Grade II', is the second annual assessment of the Government's performance across various departments. Last year's report found that the Government had been underperforming massively – and this year's follow-up will provide an update on this assessment.

Notes

1. The poll was conducted online by ICM Research on behalf of the End Violence Against Women Campaign among 524 people aged 16-20 in November 2006.
2. ICM opinion poll for Amnesty International UK of 1,095 adults in November 2005. Key findings were that between a quarter and a third of people thought a woman was sometimes to blame if she was raped if she had been drinking, flirting or was dressed in sexy clothing.

20 November 2006

⇨ The above information is reprinted with kind permission from Amnesty International UK. Visit www.amnesty.org.uk for more.

Options for domestic violence victims

Information from Citizens Advice

What is domestic violence?

Domestic violence covers a range of situations where one person in some way harms another person, with whom they have some pre-existing relationship.

Domestic violence can therefore be one person physically attacking another or it may be another form of abuse such as pestering with phone calls, installing a lover in the family home, or putting superglue in the locks of the victim's car doors.

For the above actions to be counted as domestic violence, the victim and the perpetrator must have had some form of relationship, but they do not need to be heterosexual partners and they need not live in the same property.

Options available to people affected by violence

If you are the victim of a violent relationship, get immediate practical advice on the options available, which may be to:
⇨ attempt to stop the violence and stay with the perpetrator of the violence;
⇨ leave home temporarily;
⇨ leave home permanently;
⇨ stay in the present home and get the perpetrator of the violence to leave;
⇨ take legal action.

Finding somewhere safe to stay

If you are a victim of a violent relationship you may need somewhere safe to stay, either alone or with your children. The options are:
⇨ stay at home if you think this is safe;
⇨ stay with relatives or friends;
⇨ stay in a women's refuge. This is only an option for women (with or without children);
⇨ get emergency accommodation from the local authority under homeless persons law – this will usually mean a bed and breakfast hostel;
⇨ get privately rented accommodation.

Women's Aid refuges

Women's Aid refuges are safe houses run by and for women suffering domestic violence. Refuges provide somewhere safe for women and their children to stay and allow some time and space for the woman to think about what to do next.

Staff at refuges are specialised in dealing with domestic violence, and so can give a lot of emotional and practical support, for example, advice on benefit claims, which solicitors to use and, if necessary, how to contact the police.

To find out your nearest refuge with spaces available, you should contact the National Domestic Violence helpline, (see under heading Further help). Helpline staff will do their best to find you somewhere safe to stay that night even if the local refuge is full. They are also happy to talk to women about any questions they have about refuges.

Going to the local authority, or housing executive in Northern Ireland

Your local authority may have a duty to provide you with housing if you are homeless. You will normally be considered to be legally homeless if it is not reasonable for you to occupy your home because of the risk or fear of domestic violence.

Local authorities, or housing executive in Northern Ireland, should deal sympathetically with applications from people who are in fear of violence. You can ask for a private interview, with someone of the same sex, and can take a friend with you for support.

The local authority (housing executive in Northern Ireland) may have a duty to provide interim accommodation for you while it decides whether you are legally homeless.

Going to privately rented accommodation

If you decide to go into privately rented accommodation you will be unlikely to be able to arrange it quickly. This is really only an option for people who have time to plan their departure and can afford this accommodation.

Longer-term solutions

Once you have found a safe place to stay short-term, you will need to think about what to do in the longer term. You will need to consider:

⇨ whether you wish to permanently separate from your partner. You should seek legal advice (see under heading Legal remedies and procedures);

⇨ whether you want to take action to keep the violent partner away from you. You should seek legal advice (see under heading Legal remedies and procedures);

⇨ housing. Your legal rights to the family home will depend upon the type of housing you are leaving, the legal status of your relationship and whether or not you have children. You should get legal advice to ensure that you do everything possible to protect rights to the family home. You should seek advice about the family home even if you are leaving permanently because, if your partner sells the home, you may lose money and possessions;

⇨ children. If you have children you will need to decide if you are taking the children with you. It may be unsafe to leave them behind. You may need to use the courts to resolve who the children should live with and with whom they should have contact. You should seek legal advice (see under heading Legal remedies and procedures)

⇨ money. You will need to sort out your benefit entitlement and tax arrangements and whether or not to apply to court for maintenance for yourself. You may also want to apply to the Child Support Agency for a maintenance assessment for your children. If you claim certain benefits, you will automatically be contacted by the Child Support Agency, and you should keep in mind that claiming maintenance from a violent partner could be distressing or threatening. However, you may be able to opt out if there is a risk to you or a child living with you.

If you need further information and advice you should consult an experienced adviser, for example, a solicitor, law centre or Citizens' Advice Bureau.

Legal remedies and procedures

Going to a solicitor

If you want to discuss legal protection for yourself and your children, consult a solicitor who is experienced in matrimonial work. Local Women's Aid groups, the police, rape crisis groups, or women's centres usually know of local solicitors who are both experienced and sympathetic.

There are several specialist organisations which can help violent people who want to stop being violent

---

A local advice agency, such as a law centre or Citizens' Advice Bureau, should be able to help you find a local solicitor who is experienced in this area of the law. In England and Wales, you can also look on the Community Legal Advice website at: www.communityleagaladvice.org.uk. In Scotland, go to the website of the Scottish Legal Aid Board at: www.slab.org.uk, and in Northern Ireland, go to the website of the Northern Ireland Legal Services Commission at: www.nilsc.org.uk.

You should make an appointment as soon as you feel ready, and could take someone with you for support the first time you go to the solicitor. The initial interview will probably last quite a long time, during which the solicitor should discuss with you what courses of legal action are open to you and whether you are entitled to legal aid.

If you take legal action to protect yourself or your family from domestic violence, you may qualify for legal aid without having to meet the normal financial conditions.

Perpetrators of violence

There are several specialist organisations which can help violent people who want to stop being violent. Some are self-help groups run by others who have had experience of violent behaviour, others may be run by trained counsellors. It may also be possible for you to get help through your GP.

Further help

National Domestic Violence Helpline

A national 24-hour helpline provides access to advice and support to women experiencing domestic violence. The freephone helpline number is 0808 200 0247. The helpline is provided jointly by Women's Aid and Refuge.

Women's Aid

PO Box 391
Bristol
BS99 7WS
Helpline: 0808 200 0247 (24 hours)
Tel (admin): 0117 944 4411
Fax: 0117 924 1703
E-mail: info@womensaid.org.uk
Website: www.womensaid.org.uk

The national helpline offers advice and support to women experiencing domestic violence. Women's Aid can also give details of refuges and the availability of refuge places throughout the UK. Its website provides links to specialist organisations that offer services to women from different minority ethnic communities and cultures.

Scottish Women's Aid

2nd Floor
132 Rose Street
Edinburgh
EH2 3JD
Helpline: 0800 027 1234
Tel (admin): 0131 226 6606
Fax: 0131 226 2996
Website: www.scottishwomensaid.co.uk

Scottish Domestic Abuse Helpline

Tel: 0800 027 1234
Website: www.domesticabuse.co.uk

This 24-hour domestic abuse

helpline can provide housing, legal and benefits advice for all parts of Scotland. It also provides an opportunity to discuss your problems in confidence.

Welsh Women's Aid

Cardiff National Office
38-48 Crwys Road
Cardiff
CF24 4NN
Freephone domestic abuse helpline: 0808 801 0800 (open 24 hours)
Tel: 09 2039 0874
Fax: 029 2039 0878
E-mail: KirsticPavey@welshwomensaid.org.uk
Website: www.welshwomensaid.org

Women's Aid Federation (Northern Ireland)

129 University Street
Belfast
BT7 1HP
24-hour Domestic Violence Helpline: 0800 917 1414
Tel (admin): 028 9024 9041
Website: www.niwaf.org
General e-mail: info@niwaf.org

Refuge

2/8 Maltravers Street
London
WC2R 3EE
Tel: Helpline: 0808 200 0247 (24 hours)
Tel: Admin: 020 7395 7700
E-mail: info@refuge.org.uk
Website: www.refuge.org.uk

The national helpline offers advice and support to anyone experiencing domestic violence. Refuge provides safe, emergency accommodation through a network of refuges throughout the UK. It also provides culturally-specific services for women from different minority ethnic communities and cultures. Its website has links to specialist organisations, including specialist organisations for refugees.

Rights of Women

52-54 Featherstone Street
London
EC1Y 8RT
Legal advice line: 020 7251 6577
Sexual violence advice line: 0207 251 8887
Administration: 020 7251 6575/6
Fax: 020 7490 5377
E-mail: info@row.org.uk

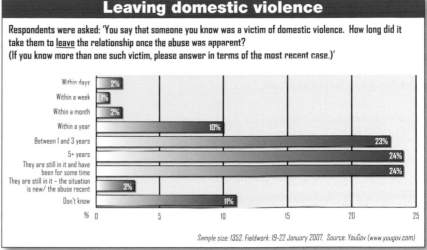

Leaving domestic violence

Respondents were asked: 'You say that someone you know was a victim of domestic violence. How long did it take them to <u>leave</u> the relationship once the abuse was apparent? (If you know more than one such victim, please answer in terms of the most recent case.)'

- Within days: 2%
- Within a week: 1%
- Within a month: 2%
- Within a year: 10%
- Between 1 and 3 years: 23%
- 5+ years: 24%
- They are still in it and have been for some time: 24%
- They are still in it – the situation is new/ the abuse recent: 3%
- Don't know: 11%

Sample size: 1352. Fieldwork: 19-22 January 2007. Source: YouGov (www.yougov.com)

Website: www.rightsofwomen.org.uk

Rights of Women is a voluntary organisation that runs a legal advice telephone line, offering confidential legal advice on domestic violence. They also run a sexual violence legal advice line. Rights of Women produce free information sheets which can be downloaded from their website.

Police domestic violence units

There are a number of police domestic violence units, which have staff specially trained to help people experiencing domestic violence. They work closely with other organisations such as local solicitors and Women's Aid groups. Your local police station, in the phone book under Police, will be able to tell you if they have a domestic violence unit, or where the nearest one is.

Survivors UK Ltd

2 Leathermarket Street
London
SE1 3HN
Tel: 0845 122 1201 (Helpline: Monday, Tuesday and Thursday, 7pm-10pm)
E-mail: info@survivorsuk.org
Website: www.survivorsuk.org

A national helpline for men who have been victims of violence, sexual assault and rape. The helpline may be able to arrange counselling or a support group if you live in the London area. If you live outside London, Survivors UK may be able to provide details of an appropriate service outside the London area.

Everyman Project

1A Waterloo Road
London
N19 5NJ
Tel: 020 7263 8884 (Helpline: Tuesday and Wednesday, 6.30pm-9pm)
E-mail: everymanproject@btopenworld.com
Website: www.everymanproject.co.uk

The Everyman Project offers counselling to men in the London area who want to change their violent or abusive behaviour. It also has a national helpline which offers advice to anyone worried about their own, or someone else's, violent or abusive behaviour.

As well as using their helpline number above, you can phone them during their office opening hours. These are Mondays 10am to 2pm, Wednesdays from 10am to 5pm and Fridays from 1pm to 5pm.

M-Power

14 Thorpe Road
Norwich
NR1 1RY
Tel: 0808 808 4321 (Thursday evenings only, 8pm-10pm)
E-mail: support@male-rape.org.uk
Website: www.male-rape.org.uk

A national helpline for men who have been raped, assaulted or abused in childhood or adult life. The helpline also supports partners (male and female) and family members of abused men.

⇨ The above information is reprinted with kind permission from Citizens Advice. Visit www.adviceguide.org.uk for more information on this and many more topics.

© Citizens Advice, an operating name of the National Association of Citizens' Advice Bureaux

Seeking help

Information from the University of Sheffield

Some facts

Cultural, social and religious norms may prevent women from seeking help for domestic abuse. This particularly affects those from religious groups, high social status women and women who have left a male partner for a lesbian relationship. These women may all feel particularly exposed to censure which impedes help-seeking behaviours.

Women from black and minority ethnic communities, and women working in prostitution also have reason to fear prejudicial attitudes and reactions, as do women with disabilities or learning difficulties.

Women who are abused are vulnerable to depression and other serious mental health problems, such as self-harm, eating disorders, attempted suicide, and they are likely to drink to excess or take drugs in order to achieve relief from the emotional as well as the physical pain.

Just basically take these and come back and see me in six weeks, not like, I can get you this help, I can get you that help, just push it behind the door and 'you're depressed, just take these tablets'. I finished up, I stopped taking them, 'cause I didn't feel any benefit whatsoever and well, they are addictive aren't they?

These factors render them less likely or willing to seek help for themselves or their children and increase their fears about being deemed an unfit mother.

That's a real problem...that fear of having your kids taken away...

Because of their mental state, women who experience domestic abuse are fearful for themselves and their children and they, like the children and young people in their care, experience long-term stress that impedes their confidence and ability to resist the abuse and seek help.

Women perceive disclosure to health and social care professionals to be a significant risk. Reporting

The University Of Sheffield.

domestic abuse puts women at further risk from the abuser. It also provides the potential for professional and public scrutiny of their lives, leading to blame, and possibly child-care proceedings, which may result in the abusive partner gaining custody.

Cultural, social and religious norms may prevent women from seeking help for domestic abuse

---

I've been in that situation and you don't phone them 'cos you're trying to battle it and keep you and your children together and all you're doing is your best not to get hit, to protect your children so they don't see it and then you get someone who comes in and all they want to know about is what's happening with the kids blah, blah blah...

It is important not to underestimate the influence of embarrassment, shame and guilt in preventing help-seeking in cases of domestic abuse.

Characteristic injuries

The physical results typical of domestic abuse are characterised by fractures, contusions, burns, dislocated joints, internal injuries and gun-shot. In the USA as many as 30% of all injuries suffered by adult women who report for treatment in accident and emergency clinics, are attributable to domestic abuse, with one in nine of these being there because of ongoing domestic abuse. Such women are

three times more likely than the non-abused women to be pregnant. Pregnant women who have been victims of domestic abuse notably report blows to the abdomen, breasts, and genitals as well as sexual assault. Thus the unborn baby as well as the mother is in danger. Women in this situation are more likely to deliver low-birth-weight infants.

In addition to physical injury, domestic abuse often has debilitating emotional consequences that may render the mother incapable of taking steps to protect both herself and her children. Primary psychiatric dysfunction such as depression, anxiety, panic attacks, eating disorders, dissociative behaviour, suicide attempts or attempts and substance abuse may all be associated with current or past domestic abuse.

What women say about seeking help: results of the interviews with the women

The women confirmed that there were many obstacles to seeking help and leaving their abusive partners. Reasons were personal such as lack of self-confidence and fear of the partner, feeling unjustified at leaving or feeling sorry for him. Many women find it difficult to name their experiences as domestic abuse at first as this woman's story shows:

In my case where there weren't a lot, well it sounds a bit contradictory cause when I listen to what I am saying it sounds like there were a lot of physical abuse, but I didn't think at the time there were a lot of physical abuse and I didn't sort of class myself as a person suffering domestic violence, just that I had got a really abusive husband, that's all. And I didn't sort of when I first started going to domestic violence project I used to feel a bit like sort of guilty, that I shouldn't be there you know? Because I had not been getting beaten up every day I thought it didn't count you know...when you leave you actually realise how bad things were.

Concerns focused on the physical danger from the abuser, the terror of having made the decision and having to act on it and then the emotional 'danger' from her own sense of humiliation:

Shame. I think that's the big one. Fear, the fact that if you do tell somebody then you have got to do something about it really. You're then put on the spot then and once you have actually declared it, off you go. I think that it's really fear from him, fear of what you are going to do when you have told. Your shame, your embarrassment I think that's probably around it really.

There were also issues about lack of trust in the law enforcement and social care services resulting in fear of disclosure. The abuser is dangerous and no one is seen as able to prevent his aggression and violence:

I'd rather have the fear of him kicking down the door any minute than him kicking down the door any minute with a charge on his head 'cos that would be worse, that would be worse.

How do women decide to disclose? Whom do you disclose to and when?

This is an important barrier:

I didn't feel like he was the right person really to speak about relationships... cause he's the doctor. I go there more for treatment if I have a stomach ache or a head ache or something like that and to say I need help with domestic... you know I feel like he is not the right person you know.

It is, however, disturbing to note that even when women take their courage in their hands and tell someone it frequently falls on deaf ears:

Question: And what was her reaction? Answer: Nothing, nothing at all, you know she just, it seemed to me that she just sort of saw this kind of thing every day you know, she just didn't seem perturbed by it all, you know she just asked me if I was alright and that I could go back if it happened again and talk to her if I wanted to, but there was no sort of referring on or anything.... so I just sort of went home and got back into it......it made it seem unimportant, you know I thought well why should I make a fuss obviously its not a big fuss you know I mean he has only bitten me.

It is widely believed that women who experience domestic violence and remain in or return to the abusive situation often fail to attract either sympathy or attention from the public, particularly if they also have children, or law enforcement agencies. Women's awareness of this is a major obstacle to their help-seeking.

We therefore conducted a survey of public opinion in order to assess how far public attitudes actually reflected that perspective.

⇨ The above information is re-printed with kind permission from the University of Sheffield. Visit www. shef.ac.uk for more information.

© *University of Sheffield*

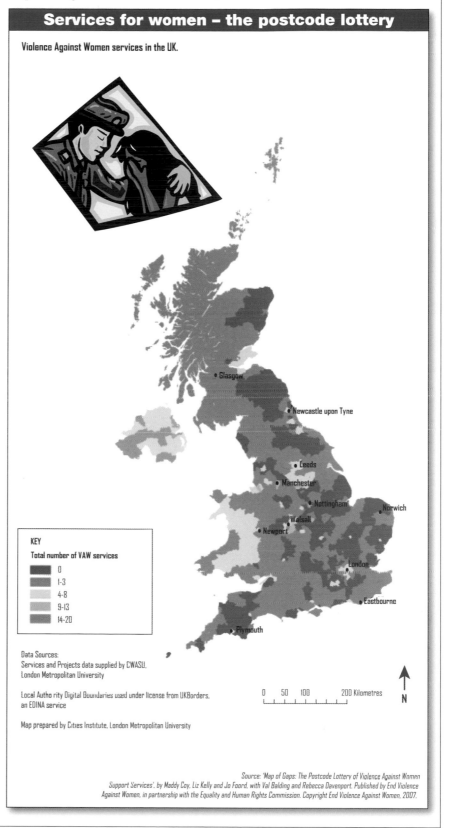

Services for women – the postcode lottery

Violence Against Women services in the UK.

KEY
Total number of VAW services
- 0
- 1-3
- 4-8
- 9-13
- 14-20

Data Sources:
Services and Projects data supplied by CWASU,
London Metropolitan University

Local Authority Digital Boundaries used under license from UKBorders, an EDINA service

Map prepared by Cities Institute, London Metropolitan University

0 50 100 200 Kilometres

N

Source: 'Map of Gaps: The Postcode Lottery of Violence Against Women Support Services', by Maddy Coy, Liz Kelly and Jo Foord, with Val Balding and Rebecca Davenport. Published by End Violence Against Women, in partnership with the Equality and Human Rights Commission. Copyright End Violence Against Women, 2007.

When violence first hit home

Wife-beating was still being joked about at dinner parties when a squalid house in Chiswick opened its doors to women fleeing abusive partners. Ros Taylor looks at the refuge movement today as it marks its 35th anniversary

The memory of one woman whose husband had taken a hammer and chisel to her face still haunts Sandra Horley, chief executive of the charity Refuge. 'He had broken her jaw in five places and she needed 250 stitches,' she says. 'Her face was a mass of purple bruising; you couldn't see a square of normal skin colour. I had to feed her liquids through a straw.'

Horley's memory bank no doubt contains many hundreds of such horrific stories. This month marks the 35th anniversary of the charity that she has run for more than two decades. An organisation that has achieved the inestimable feat of bringing the scourge of domestic violence to popular attention and understanding, it has also provided help, care and security to many thousands of women and children who have been living in fear of familial violence - and even death. Women who have had their teeth knocked out, who have been throttled, punched and burnt, who have been thrown down stairs and verbally abused until any confidence they may have had is shredded. Given the changed social attitudes that Refuge has nurtured, it is shocking to recall how dismissive people were about domestic violence even just a few decades ago.

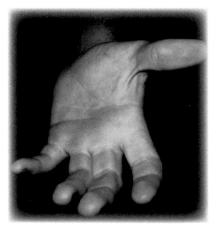

Although the women's movement was firmly established by the late 1970s, wife-beating was still regularly joked about at dinner parties. 'I dreaded telling people what I did for a living,' says Horley, because the myths surrounding domestic violence were so pervasive. Women who called the police were simply advised to make it up with their husband or partner. 'You absolutely could not get the police to attend incidents for love or money. Nothing happened.'

Although the women's movement was firmly established by the late 1970s, wife-beating was still regularly joked about at dinner parties

---

It is no exaggeration, then, to say that, until Chiswick Women's Aid, the forerunner of Refuge, began to offer women sanctuary, the concept of domestic violence - as opposed to wife-beating - was unheard of. The idea that this could take the form of emotional, as well as physical, abuse, and that children could also be victims, would have been derided. Hardly anyone would have predicted that 35 years later a Home Office paper would describe it as a 'horrendous crime'.

In some ways, though, the movement got off to an inauspicious start. In late 1971, Erin Pizzey - a bored thirtysomething housewife who would soon become an outspoken writer and campaigner - was running a women's group from a house in Belmont Terrace, Chiswick. When a bruised woman turned up on her doorstep and said that no one would help her, Pizzey agreed to take her in. Many others soon followed.

By 1974 the managing director of the building company Bovis had offered her the much bigger house where Horley came to work in 1983. 'I remember being astonished that first day,' she says. The building was supposed to house 35 women, but the open-door policy meant it sometimes accommodated four times that number. 'There were rats, graffiti all over the walls. It was straight out of Dickens. I was so distressed by the rats I rang up environmental health and asked them what to do.' Horley was no ingénue. When she answered the job ad to take over the refuge she had already worked at another shelter, the Haven in Wolverhampton. Still, she was shocked. 'It wasn't a squat, but it was squalid,' she remembers. But women fleeing their violent partners were so desperate they were undeterred by the vermin and the overcrowding. 'There were hundreds of women ringing. We could never meet the demand.'

Refuge has always been committed to assisting every woman who sought its help. But it suffered a setback in the late 1970s when Pizzey began suggesting that many victims unconsciously enjoyed violence, dividing them into 'genuine battered women' and 'violence-prone women'. In her controversial book *Prone to Violence*, she described how one woman who sought her help repeatedly 'needed murder games to feel alive'. When her son was taken into care, she begged Pizzey to vouch for her fitness to look after him. 'I can't,' Pizzey told her. 'If you can't come to terms with your own need for violence, he's safer away from you. But you don't want to give it up. I'm sorry, love.' Pizzey was reviled. Many declared her a traitor, undermining the very cause she pioneered. She left Chiswick Women's Aid in 1981. 'On the positive side,' says Horley, carefully, 'one has to give her a great deal of credit for setting up the movement in the first place.' But Pizzey's theories, she says, are misguided. 'There is no evidence whatsoever to support her theory ... It is a total myth that women like, or seek, violence and it is wrong to judge those who are forced to return to an abusive man – they may simply have no other option.' Today, the number of women calling the hotline, run jointly by Refuge and Women's Aid, continues to rise and each year around 63,000 women and children are admitted to a refuge. Refuge's 30 hostels house a core group of around 25 to 35 women and the charity needs £10,000 a day for running costs.

One of the women who sought help in recent years was Laura, whose partner first attacked her – completely out of the blue – while she was driving him to his Sunday football game. He turned around and punched her directly in the face when she explained that she didn't know where he was playing. After that, the violence escalated – with incidents including strangulation. Laura contacted Refuge after one of the incidents in which her partner pushed her – his attacks were so frequent that she has had to have physiotherapy for the scar tissue formed in her thigh from the repeated falls (the wounds were compounded by him kicking her). During their relationship, Laura had lost much of her confidence, and had once attempted an overdose, but, with help from Refuge, she was able to leave her partner and start anew. Although she still lives in fear of him – constantly looking over her shoulder – she has built a successful career.

Hostels are still key, but they are no longer the only option. The Domestic Violence Crime and Victims Act 2004 makes it an offence to breach a 'no molestation order', but despite this, many perpetrators are able to find out where their ex-partner is living and try to return. Some local authorities run 'sanctuary schemes', reinforcing one of the rooms in an abused woman's house so she can retreat and lock and bolt the door.

Since Horley began her work, the attitudes of the police have fundamentally changed – just yesterday 500 Metropolitan Police officers made raids across London, targeting domestic violence and hate crimes, co-ordinated to draw attention to just how seriously these offences are now taken. Of those now arrested, more than a third are charged and a further 15% cautioned. Despite what Horley calls a 'postcode lottery', the criminal justice system recognises domestic violence and is beginning to act. Yet two women still die each week in England and Wales at the hands of a partner or ex-partner, a figure that has barely altered since 1997. Horley is fully aware that a refuge is an escape and not a solution. 'It's about power ... men beat women up because they get away with it. We could have a refuge on every corner but as long as society continues to hide, excuse and ignore domestic violence, it will carry on behind closed doors.'

1 December 2006

Information for perpetrators

Information from Men's Advice Line (MALE)

Although the MALE project is primarily aimed at supporting male victims, we regularly receive calls from men who are concerned, or have concerns, about their own abusive behaviour and violence towards their partners and/or children.

If you would like to speak to someone about your behaviour, please contact Respect on 0845 122 8609 (Monday, Tuesday, Wednesday and Friday 10am-1pm and 2pm-5pm). Website: www.respect.uk.net

Perpetrator programmes
Victims of violence are not the only people that need help – those responsible are usually desperate to change. If you are such a person here is an overview of what help is available to you – and what will be covered if you refer to a suitable programme.

Perpetrator programmes are designed to help men to change their behaviour

---

Overview of perpetrator programmes
Perpetrator programmes are designed to help men to change their behaviour and develop respectful, non-abusive relationships. Most perpetrator programmes work with men and occasionally with women.

They're usually small groups of 8-15 men who have been violent or abusive in a current or previous relationship. They generally include a wide range of men of all races, classes and backgrounds.

What do perpetrator programmes involve?
The groups are usually run by two or three experienced group-workers – at least one man and at least one woman. There are many different programmes across the UK, and the content will vary, but on the whole they will cover these issues:
⇨ What is violence and abuse?

⇨ Understanding why I'm violent.

⇨ Learning that I am in control of my own behaviour and can choose not to be violent.

⇨ Taking responsibility for my behaviour, without blaming others or minimising it.

⇨ Understanding the impact of violence and abuse on my partner and children.

⇨ Learning how to notice when I am becoming abusive – and how to stop.

⇨ Learning different, non-abusive ways of dealing with difficulties in my relationship.

⇨ Dealing non-abusively with my partner's anger.

⇨ Recognising how I get wound up – and learning how to wind myself down.

⇨ Negotiation and listening – how to build a respectful relationship.

⇨ Some groups are discussion based, but most use a variety of interactive exercises to make the learning realistic, stimulating and relevant to men's own situations.

⇨ Most programmes will have a check-in round where each man is asked to report any violence or abuse he has used since the last group and any difficulties or problems in his relationship he wants to raise. The emphasis of this round, as with the whole programme, should be on safety.

How long do they last for?

Programmes will differ in length and content, but Respect's guidelines recommend the following:

⇨ Changing behaviour is a long-term process – especially for someone who has used violence and abuse for a long time. Programmes should be at least 75 hours – usually this will mean that each client attends at least 24 weekly sessions of 2-3 hours.

⇨ Each group session will have a particular theme (see the list above). Some themes will last over several weeks.

⇨ Some groups will be closed – this means that all the clients join at the same time and complete the group together. Others will be rolling programmes – where there is a constant influx of new clients who join every 4-6 weeks.

How can you join?

Some programmes take men who self-refer, some take men who are mandated to attend by the courts as part of a probation order, or as a recommendation from the family courts. Respect will be able to tell you which programmes take self-referrals.

Men who refer themselves will generally meet with a worker for an assessment interview. This is to enable both the worker and the client to check that the programme is suitable and to sign a contract. Once a man is accepted onto a programme he will usually join a group at the next intake session.

How can I find out about perpetrator programmes in my local area?

Unfortunately, not every area in the UK has a perpetrator programme. For details on the nearest programme to you, call the Respect Phoneline, a service run by Respect – the UK association for domestic violence perpetrator programmes and associated support services – on 0845 122 8609 Monday, Tuesday, Wednesday and Friday 10am to 1pm and 2pm to 5pm or go to www. respect.uk.net. The phoneline is an information line and does not provide counselling or emotional support.

What about support for women?

Any woman whose partner or ex-partner is attending a domestic violence perpetrator programme will have experienced some level of violence or abuse and for most this will have been over a long time.

It is extremely important that these women are offered support to help them deal with the often devastating effects of this violence. Most perpetrator programmes offer (and Respect recommends) a separate and confidential support service for the women partners and ex-partners of the men they are working with.

Do the programmes work?

It is the man himself who is responsible for his behaviour – no programme can guarantee that he will / has changed or will be safe. Unfortunately it's impossible to predict exactly which men will change and which won't – or how much. Some will change a lot, some a bit and some not at all.

As there are no guarantees about which men will change, it is crucial that the focus of programmes is not on men changing, but on women and children being safer. So, even if he doesn't change, the perpetrator programme can ensure that steps are taken to protect his partner by working closely with the women's support service and other agencies.

How are perpetrator programmes different from anger management groups?

Anger management groups usually teach short-term techniques to help individuals modify their reactions to chronic feelings of anger, whereas domestic violence perpetrator programmes are targeted at those who have a problem with violence towards their partner. While many abusive men describe themselves as having a problem controlling their anger, in cases of domestic violence anger is not the issue.

⇨ Domestic violence perpetrators are extremely selective about who they behave violently towards and the level of severity of that violence. They might feel angry at their boss, their father, their partner – but only choose to use violence against their partner. Rather than being out of control, their behaviour is about controlling.

⇨ Not all of men's violence is about anger. Abusive men learn to label all powerful emotional states as anger, when in fact they also experience more vulnerable feelings of fear, hurt, powerlessness and betrayal.

⇨ So for example if she has come home late he might feel a mixture of feelings – worry, upset, jealousy – as well as anger. Perpetrator programmes explore the underlying emotions and thoughts at the time of an assault rather than address control of the mislabelled anger.

⇨ Information from Men's Advice Line. Please visit www.mensadviceline. org.uk for more information.

© Men's Advice Line (MALE)

Pledge to cut domestic violence 'has failed'

By Jamie Doward

The government stands accused of failing in its pledges to tackle domestic abuse after it emerged that fewer than half of all men ordered to attend specialist programmes aimed at curbing their violent behaviour complete them.

It has also been forced to admit that it has yet to implement a high-profile plan to place men who beat their partners under restraint orders, despite announcing the scheme more than three years ago.

Fewer than half of all men ordered to attend specialist programmes aimed at curbing their violent behaviour complete them

Opposition politicians were quick to accuse the government of failing to live up to its promises, as probation teams across Britain highlighted problems with the Integrated Domestic Abuse Programme. In one case, a man from South Wales found guilty of choking his wife repeated the offence after more than a year waiting to go on the programme.

Probation officers in the region say they now have more than 40 men waiting for courses, a picture their union, Napo, say is reflected across the UK.

West Midlands probation officers say their backlog is now so serious they are placing only the most high-risk abusers on the programmes. In Avon and Somerset, waiting lists are between eight and 12 months and in Yorkshire some offenders have been waiting for up to two years.

The programmes run for up to 27 weeks and cost between £8,000 and £10,000 each. Extremely popular with the courts, police and the Crown Prosecution Service, they were introduced in 2001 and widely promoted by the government in 2005 as part of its National Domestic Violence Plan. But the Ministry of Justice confirmed that only 1,800 out of more than 4,000 handed down by the courts in 2007 were completed.

In 2004, the then Home Secretary, David Blunkett, promised the Domestic Violence Crime and Victims Bill, which introduced specialist Domestic Violence Courts to expand the use of domestic abuse programmes, was 'the biggest shake-up of domestic violence legislation for 30 years'. And in 2006 Home Office minister Vernon Coaker pledged that the government would 'place [domestic abuse] victims at the heart of the criminal justice system... while bringing perpetrators to account for their offences'.

Harry Fletcher, Napo's assistant director-general, said: 'The government has widely flagged dealing with domestic violence as a central plank of its policy. There are now, disturbingly, cases of further offences of domestic violence being perpetrated by men awaiting the course.'

A Ministry of Justice spokeswoman confirmed that in some areas demand for the domestic abuse programmes was 'outstripping' places, but that the government was tackling the problem: 'We are refining the process of assessing offenders to ensure that only those who will benefit from an intensive programme are recommended for it.'

The government has also yet to implement measures introduced in 2005 that would allow courts to impose restraint orders against men suspected of beating their partners even if they have not been convicted.

'They were introduced with great fanfare as an urgent measure to better control domestic violence,' said Edward Garnier MP, the Conservative's Justice spokesman and a Crown Court Recorder. 'But the government simply hasn't implemented the legislation.' A Home Office spokesman said 'discussions' about implementing the restraint orders were 'ongoing'.

17 February 2008

↳ This article first appeared in *The Observer.*

DO YOU THINK THE GOVERNMENT WILL INTRODUCE RESTRAINT ORDERS BEFORE OR AFTER HE BREAKS MY OTHER ARM?

Rise in domestic violence convictions

CPS domestic violence figures show further rise in convictions

The Crown Prosecution Service's latest figures for domestic violence show that convictions are continuing to rise year on year and have risen by 20 per cent since 2003. Three-quarters of the cases in the Crown Courts – where the most serious cases are heard – ended in a conviction.

The figures were released in the annual CPS snapshot survey which counted and analysed the number of cases of domestic violence finalised in December 2006. This is the fifth and final snapshot of domestic violence cases the CPS has carried out since 2002. The snapshot will be replaced in 2008-09 with an annual Hate Crimes Report.

Director of Public Prosecutions, Sir Ken Macdonald, QC, said: 'These figures show the huge amount of work everyone has put over the past five years to make sure cases are prosecuted more and more successfully. Domestic violence victims are receiving a better service and better care in the criminal justice system than ever before.

'This 2006 snapshot reflects the national picture across the CPS. There is an increase in cases, which shows victims have more confidence in the system. We have also seen an increase in successful outcomes and the CPS is dropping fewer cases.'

Conviction rates have risen from their lowest recorded point of 46 per cent in 2003, to 59 per cent in 2005, up to 66 per cent in 2006 – a-year-on year improvement of seven per cent and 20 per cent over three years.

Key findings in the survey included:

⇨ Recorded cases of domestic violence increased by three per cent compared with December 2005, to more than 3,100 cases charged for prosecution; double those recorded in 2002.

⇨ Magistrates' courts had a conviction rate of 64 per cent and Crown Courts had a conviction rate of 75 per cent.

⇨ Fewer cases were discontinued by the CPS: 17 per cent in 2003, 13 per cent in 2005 and 11 per cent in 2006.

⇨ There was a fall in the number of victims who retracted their statement. In 2004 it was 34 per cent and this fell to 28 per cent in 2006.

Sir Ken said: 'I am determined that the improvements highlighted in this report will continue. During 2007 and 2008, we will focus on driving up performance still further. We are aiming at a new target of 70 per cent successful prosecutions by April 2008.'

The Crown Prosecution Service's latest figures for domestic violence show that convictions are continuing to rise year on year and have risen by 20 per cent since 2003

Commenting on the CPS snapshot, Baroness Scotland, QC, Attorney General, said: 'Domestic violence is a terrible crime. Victims are attacked in what should be the safety of their own home by someone who should care for them. Domestic violence accounts for about 15 per cent of violent incidents. Clearly it is a crime that we should all be concerned about.

'The Crown Prosecution Service plays a key role in protecting the victims of domestic violence and bringing their attackers to justice. I am therefore extremely pleased to see that the CPS is bringing more cases of domestic violence to court and that more attackers are being convicted.'

Sandra Horley OBE, Chief executive of national domestic violence charity Refuge, commented: 'Refuge is encouraged to see the rising number of convictions for domestic violence. As the most abhorrent of crimes, it is vital that domestic violence is taken seriously and perpetrators held accountable for their actions. The legal system is often complex,

intimidating and isolating for victims of domestic violence, but Specialist Domestic Violence Courts are having a positive impact. Thanks in many cases to the support of independent domestic violence advocates, the number of women giving evidence is increasing.'

There have been a number of initiatives during the year since the last CPS domestic violence report was published. These have included an increase in the number of Specialist Domestic Violence Courts to 64; a CPS poster campaign about violence against women highlighting the range of offences which could be prosecuted as well as support services for victims; the revision of the CPS employee domestic violence policy; and more than 2,800 CPS staff have been trained in domestic violence issues since April 2005, including all lawyers who prosecute in the specialist domestic violence courts.

Case studies

Humberside: A victim was kicked in the stomach by her partner in an attempt to 'kick her baby out of her' – he wanted to get her back on the streets working as a prostitute for him. She did not provide a statement but gave very early/immediate accounts to her midwife, social worker, family and the police – her accounts were entirely consistent on each occasion

and were consistent with her injuries. The CPS charged and ran the case on the basis of hearsay evidence and bad character evidence. The victim was entirely supported by the police/ WCU and domestic violence support worker. About a month or so before the trial, the victim decided of her own volition that she would give a statement after all. She did so and on the day of trial the defendant pleaded guilty – he was sentenced to a total of five years' imprisonment.

West Yorkshire: The victim made an original complaint to the police of common assault. However, she later became reconciled with her partner and refused to give evidence. The police had obtained photographs of the injuries and there were limited admissions during the interview. The trial proceeded on the basis of self-defence and whether the defendant's actions were disproportionate. The defendant was convicted and given a community-based sentence. The whole case took just nine weeks from assault to trial to sentence.

London: The victim was the girlfriend of the defendant. She had only been in the country for five months and they had been together for three months. An argument ensued about her talking too loudly on the phone whilst he was watching television. He punched her in the

face and beat her with a belt causing lash marks on her back. There was a previous incident of violence, which the victim had been too scared to report. He was arrested and interviewed and denied hitting her with his hands but said that he had whipped her with a belt in 'self-defence'. He could not explain why the marks were on her back. She had to move in to a refuge, as she had nowhere else to go. He was charged with common assault and pleaded not guilty. The victim withdrew the allegations as she wanted to resume her relationship. The CPS decided to proceed without her evidence, on the basis of the admissions in interview and the evidence of her injuries and the fact that the defence of 'self-defence' was unlikely to be believed given that she had injuries to her back. The defendant pleaded guilty on the day of trial. He was sentenced to a two-year community rehabilitation order with a condition to attend a domestic violence perpetrators' programme. He was also ordered to pay £200 compensation to his victim.
18 July 2007

⇨ The above information is reprinted with kind permission from the Crown Prosecution Service. Visit www.cps.gov.uk for more information.

So what's the point of going to court?

Two horrific domestic violence cases – involving beating, branding and slashing – resulted in small fines for the men found guilty this week. Why is the legal system still failing women, asks Emine Saner

Some decisions are very difficult to understand, however much you analyse them. It is quite hard, for instance, to fathom what the magistrates who gave Stuart Brown a £500 fine this week – after he dragged his wife out of bed and punched her at least 24 times – meant when they described him as being of 'good character'. For the seven years of their marriage, Brown's wife, Carol

McEwan, complained of regular verbal and physical abuse. Brown hasn't even lost his job – he still works at the Norwich and Norfolk University Hospital as a consultant anaesthetist, although the General Medical Council will be holding a disciplinary hearing. 'No punishment this court could enforce could come anywhere near the impact you feel this had on you, your profession and your

colleagues,' the presiding magistrate, John Warne, told Brown.

The case caps a week of astonishment and despair for campaigners against domestic violence. On Monday, Colin Read, a management consultant, was fined just £2,000 for a catalogue of violence against his wife, Elizabeth Axe. Read became violent soon after the couple married last year, and, in one of the worst attacks, slashed his wife's feet with a knife while she was asleep because she hadn't made his sandwiches for work the next day. When she protested, he punched her. Eight days later, he complained that she hadn't ironed one of his shirts and branded her twice with the iron on her back – the steam holes were burnt into her skin. Too terrified to see a doctor, Axe treated her burns by standing under a cold shower.

Read wasn't given a community punishment as the judge said that the demands of his job meant he would be 'too busy' to fulfil it. 'A fine is not really a deterrent,' said Axe after the three-day trial. 'People might think they can do whatever they want, pay a few pounds and it's all over.' When you consider these men's salaries, it becomes even clearer that the fines handed down were no real punishment – Brown is said to earn £100,000 a year, Read £90,000.

Axe was too afraid to go to the police – who were alerted by her friends – and had to be persuaded to go to court. After the trial she summed up her despair: 'I didn't really want to go to court. Now with the sentence the way it was, it doesn't really seem there was much point.' She has recently filed for divorce.

'These cases make a mockery of police and crown prosecution efforts to take domestic violence seriously,' says Sandra Horley from the charity Refuge. 'What is the point of the government passing new legislation if judges do not sentence in accordance with the crime? It is most worrying that non-custodial sentences appear to be the norm.'

Deborah McIlveen of the charity Women's Aid agrees. 'It takes an enormous amount of courage for a woman to prosecute her abuser in court and sentences like these may deter other women from doing so.'

One in four women in the UK experience domestic violence during their lives, and it accounts for the murders of two women – and as many as 10 suicides – a week. In Britain, police receive half a million complaints a year, although this is, of course, a tiny proportion of the actual number of incidents. The Crown Prosecution Service (CPS) says it takes domestic violence 'very seriously' and points to the increasing number of specialist prosecutors working on domestic violence cases. Overall conviction rates are higher year on year, but, looking at this week's cases, that seems almost irrelevant if the punishment doesn't fit the crime. In cases where domestic violence hasn't ended in murder, just 4% of men who are convicted serve prison sentences.

Is the criminal justice system failing domestic abuse survivors?

'[You need to look at] what you are trying to achieve when you sentence someone,' says Kevin McCormack, head of the Sentencing Guideline Secretariat. 'It can be punishment but you're also trying to make sure that it doesn't happen again. If the court reached the view that, in a particular case, there was little risk of it happening again because the relationship had ended, and if there were other things ... in the defendant's favour, then that could persuade the court to use financial penalty instead of a community or custodial sentence.'

When setting fines, he says, 'it is a balance between the seriousness of the offence and the financial resources of the individual ... £500 is quite a high fine in terms of the average level. It depends on the individual's income.' And Brown's high salary? McCormack says he won't comment on individual cases.

In Read's case, he was spared a community sentence because the judge said he was unlikely to reoffend. This will hopefully be the case, but there's no guarantee and this assumption seems yet another example of the courts' failure to understand domestic violence and its perpetrators. 'Only 24% of domestic violence survivors report to justice agencies and only a small percentage of these go forward for prosecution,' says McIlveen. 'This means that most perpetrators are not held accountable for their violent behaviour and it is most likely that they will continue to use violence. There is anecdotal evidence that when one woman escapes a violent partner, he does the same to his next partner.'

So why is the judicial system still failing women? Ranjit Kaur, director of the voluntary organisation Rights of Women, says that, historically, the law has been written from the perspective of men and is still dominated by attitudes that fail women. 'We still have judges making all sorts of comments which imply the woman is at fault, which takes us back to the time when men were allowed to beat their wives. There needs to be more training for all those involved in the criminal justice system.'

This includes the police. 'The caution rate for domestic violence perpetrators is worryingly high, despite guidance from the Association of Chief Police Officers, which recommends caution in only the minority of cases,' says Horley. 'A caution is not enough. We know that rigorous arresting, charging and sentencing, in accordance with the crime, can act as an effective deterrent. Yet the efforts of the CPS are in danger of being undermined by courts opting against custodial sentences, sometimes in favour of anger management programmes.'

Refuge seriously questions the effectiveness of these programmes. 'Little is being done to increase the number of cases brought to prosecution in the first place. This leaves thousands of women and children unprotected and living in the terrifying grip of violence in the home. More needs to be done to encourage these women to call for help. And, when they do, they must be taken seriously.'

24 August 2007

© Guardian Newspapers Limited 2007

Domestic violence register called for

Information from Emergency Services News

The Association of Chief Police Officers has said that abusive partners, men or women, should be listed on a domestic violence register similar to the sex offenders' list, and that doing so could save dozens of lives.

Chief Constable Brian Moore, APCO's spokesman on domestic violence, told MPs that, while the charity Victim Support helped more than 400,000 victims of domestic violence a year, research indicated that the true level of abuse amounted to a 'huge' 13m incidents a year.

> ### The Association of Chief Police Officers has said that abusive partners, men or women, should be listed on a domestic violence register similar to the sex offenders' list

Giving evidence to the Commons home affairs committee, which is carrying out an inquiry into domestic violence, Moore said: 'There is no domestic violence abuse register on which perpetrators should be placed.

'I think it should be given considerable extra thought by virtue of the marked correlation between domestic violence and homicide or serious violence.

'Those who go from relationship to relationship across boundaries should be subject to amenable and proportionate tracking.'

Moore said that, without a register, sharing between agencies was 'inadequate'.

'Each agency may have part of the picture. But it is only when all these pieces of information come together from police, education, social services and from housing authorities that we have the clearest picture of those at risk.

> ### While the charity Victim Support helped more than 400,000 victims of domestic violence a year, research indicated that the true level of abuse amounted to a 'huge' 13m incidents a year

'The law in this regard is inadequate. The law on information sharing is passive – there is no obligation to share when someone is at risk.

'We have to act now because year on year other people are losing their lives because of this gap in the law.'

Moore said the Home Office was adopting a wait-and-see policy and that ministers did not seem to want to change the law.

'I wish I could share their optimism,' he said.

'There are thousands of protocols about sharing information. Thousands of protocols must tell you that there is no clear system.

'We are not optimistic that, given the number of people who die each year as a result of domestic abuse, we can wait for some undefined period.' Moore believes the number of deaths from domestic violence each year could be halved if we adopted better data-sharing methods.

The Crown Prosecution Service's domestic violence implementation manager, June Watson, told the committee that latest figures showed specialist courts set up to deal with domestic violence were achieving 'successful outcomes' in 70% of cases, a better result than other courts.

24 January 2008

⇨ The above information is reprinted with kind permission from Emergency Services News. Visit their website at www.esnews.co.uk for more information.

© Emergency Services News

KEY FACTS

⇨ Domestic violence is very common: research shows that it affects one in four women in their lifetime. Two women a week are killed by their partners or former partners. All forms of domestic violence – psychological, financial, emotional and physical – come from the abuser's desire for power and control over an intimate partner or other family members. (page 1)

⇨ Blaming their behaviour on someone else, or on the relationship, their childhood, their ill health, or their alcohol or drug addiction is one way in which many abusers try to avoid personal responsibility for their behaviour. (page 2)

⇨ There are many myths and stereotypes about domestic violence, which are untrue and often deeply unfair to the women who are suffering domestic violence. These attitudes, often from those who have no experience of domestic violence, can add to a woman's feelings of despair and isolation and make it more difficult for her to seek help. (page 3)

⇨ The British Crime Survey (BCS) found that 34 per cent of women, and 62 per cent of men who had suffered domestic abuse since they were 16 years of age have probably never told anyone other than the survey in question. (page 5)

⇨ Women do not seek out relationships with violent men. Frequently, men who will become violent do not reveal this aspect of their behaviour until the relationship has become well established. In fact, for many women, the violence does not start until their first pregnancy. (page 7)

⇨ More than eight million people are victims of domestic abuse, the British Medical Association has reported. (page 10)

⇨ Although research shows that domestic violence affects mostly women, current statistics show that one in six men will be affected at some point in their lifetime. The British Crime Survey revealed that 19% of domestic violence incidents were reported to be male victims, with just under half of these having a female abuser. (page 12)

⇨ More work is needed to raise awareness of domestic abuse in same-sex relationships, according to a new study. (page 13)

⇨ Spyware is becoming a tool of domestic abuse, according to security researchers. (page 15)

⇨ The definition of domestic abuse includes forced marriage. (page 16)

⇨ A report has found that the experience of watching, hearing or otherwise being aware of domestic violence can impact children's physical, emotional and social development, both during childhood and later in life. (page 19)

⇨ 29% of women and 18% of men aged 16 to 59 reported that they had experienced one or more types of abuse (non-sexual abuse such as use of physical force, being prevented from having money or seeing friends or being belittled, sexual assault and stalking) at the hands of a current or former partner at some time since age 16. (page 24)

⇨ Only 48% of men and 60% of women surveyed by YouGov recognised that a partner limiting another's financial freedom was a form of domestic violence. (page 25)

⇨ A new ICM survey commissioned by the End Violence Against Women campaign (EVAW) has found that 42% of young people know girls whose boyfriends have hit them and that 40% know girls whose boyfriends have coerced or pressurised them to have sex. (page 26)

⇨ 24% of people surveyed by YouGov who knew someone who had been a victim of domestic violence said that it had taken the person five years or more to leave the abusive situation. A further 24% said that the abused person was still in their abusive relationship and had been for some time. (page 29)

⇨ Cultural, social and religious norms may prevent women from seeking help for domestic abuse. This particularly affects those from religious groups, high social status women and women who have left a male partner for a lesbian relationship. (page 30)

⇨ The government stands accused of failing in its pledges to tackle domestic abuse after it emerged that fewer than half of all men ordered to attend specialist programmes aimed at curbing their violent behaviour complete them. (page 35)

⇨ The Crown Prosecution Service's latest figures for domestic violence show that convictions are continuing to rise year on year and have risen by 20 per cent since 2003. Three-quarters of the cases in the Crown Courts - where the most serious cases are heard - ended in a conviction. (page 36)

⇨ The Association of Chief Police Officers has said that abusive partners, men or women, should be listed on a domestic violence register similar to the sex offenders' list, and that doing so could save dozens of lives. (page 39)

GLOSSARY

Domestic abuse
An incident of physical, sexual, emotional or financial abuse that takes place within an intimate relationship. Domestic abuse can be perpetrated by a spouse, partner or other family member and occurs regardless of gender, sex, race, class or religion. Although the majority of domestic abuse victims are women, men can also be affected. Research shows that domestic abuse will affect one in four women in their lifetime.

Emotional abuse
Emotional abuse refers to a victim being verbally attacked, criticised and put down. With frequent exposure to this behaviour, over time the victim's mental well-being suffers as their self-esteem is destroyed and the perpetrator's control over them increases. They may suffer from feelings of worthlessness, believing that they deserve the abuse or that if they were to leave the abuser, they would never find another partner and are afraid to be alone. A victim may also have been convinced by her abuser that the abuse is her fault. The abuser can use these feelings to manipulate the victim.

Forced marriage
A marriage that takes place without the consent of one or both parties. Forced marriage is not the same as an arranged marriage, which is organised by family or friends but which both parties freely enter into.

Honour crime
An honour crime or killing occurs when family members take action against a relative who is thought to have brought shame on the family. The victims are usually women who are accused of dishonouring their family by breaking their rules or going against their wishes (for example, by fleeing a forced marriage).

Perpetrator programme
A rehabilitation programme for perpetrators of domestic abuse to help them understand and try to change their abusive behaviour. The programmes are usually run with groups of 8 to 15 men who may have self-referred, or have been required to attend by a court.

Physical abuse
Physical abuse involves the use of violence or force against a victim and can include hitting, slapping, kicking, pushing, strangling or other forms of physical violence. Physical assault is a crime and the police have the power to protect victims, but in a domestic violence situation it can often take a long time for the violence to come to light. Some victims are too afraid to go to the police, believe they can reform the abuser (who they may still love), or have normalised their abusive situation and do not realise they can get help.

Refuge
A shelter, or safe house, offering a place for victims of domestic violence and their children to stay. Refuges can provide practical advice as well as emotional support for victims of domestic abuse until they can find somewhere more permanent to stay.

Sexual abuse
Sexual abuse occurs when a victim is forced into a sexual activity against their will, through violence or intimidation. Sexual abuse is always a crime, no matter what the relationship is between the victim and perpetrator. If the abuser is the partner or spouse of his victim, this does not mean he has any rights over her sexually – marital rape was criminalised in 1991.

Spyware
Spyware is a term for computer software which can be used to invade a person's privacy by monitoring their phone calls or online activities. Although usually associated with fraudsters trying to discover someone's financial details, this type of software could also be used by domestic abusers as a method of spying on and controlling their partner.

INDEX

Additional Resources

Other Issues titles

If you are interested in researching further some of the issues raised in *Domestic Abuse*, you may like to read the following titles in the **Issues** series:

⇨ Vol. 154 *The Gender Gap* (ISBN 978 1 86168 441 7)

⇨ Vol. 143 *Problem Drinking* (ISBN 978 1 86168 409 7)

⇨ Vol. 137 *Crime and Anti-Social Behaviour* (ISBN 978 1 86168 441 7)

⇨ Vol. 136 *Self-Harm* (ISBN 978 1 86168 388 5)

⇨ Vol. 133 *Teen Pregnancy and Lone Parents* (ISBN 978 1 86168 379 3)

⇨ Vol. 132 *Child Abuse* (ISBN 978 1 86168 378 6)

⇨ Vol. 130 *Homelessness* (ISBN 978 1 86168 376 2)

⇨ Vol. 125 *Understanding Depression* (ISBN 978 1 86168 364 9)

⇨ Vol. 124 *Parenting Issues* (ISBN 978 1 86168 363 2)

⇨ Vol. 122 *Bullying* (ISBN 978 1 86168 361 8)

⇨ Vol. 120 *The Human Rights Issue* (ISBN 978 1 86168 353 3)

⇨ Vol. 117 *Self-Esteem and Body Image* (ISBN 978 1 86168 350 2)

⇨ Vol. 115 *Racial Discrimination* (ISBN 978 1 86168 348 9)

⇨ Vol. 114 *Drug Abuse* (ISBN 978 1 86168 347 2)

⇨ Vol. 106 *Trends in Marriage* (ISBN 978 1 86168 326 7)

For more information about these titles, visit our website at www.independence.co.uk/publicationslist

Useful organisations

You may find the websites of the following organisations useful for further research:

⇨ **Amnesty International UK:** www.amnesty.org.uk

⇨ **British Medical Association:** www.bma.org.uk

⇨ **Citizens Advice:** www.adviceguide.org.uk

⇨ **Crown Prosecution Service:** www.cps.gov.uk

⇨ **End the Fear:** www.endthefear.org.uk

⇨ **The Hideout:** www.thehideout.org.uk

⇨ **iVillage UK:** www.iVillage.co.uk

⇨ **Lone Parents:** www.lone-parents.org.uk

⇨ **Manchester City Council:** www.manchester.gov.uk

⇨ **Men's Advice Line (MALE):** www.mensadviceline.org.uk

⇨ **Metropolitan Police Service:** www.met.police.uk

⇨ **NSPCC:** www.nspcc.org.uk

⇨ **TheSite:** www.thesite.org

⇨ **UNICEF:** www.unicef.org

⇨ **University of Bristol:** www.bris.ac.uk

⇨ **University of Sheffield:** www.shef.ac.uk

⇨ **Women's Aid:** www.womensaid.org.uk

⇨ **YouGov:** www.yougov.com

ACKNOWLEDGEMENTS

The publisher is grateful for permission to reproduce the following material.

While every care has been taken to trace and acknowledge copyright, the publisher tenders its apology for any accidental infringement or where copyright has proved untraceable. The publisher would be pleased to come to a suitable arrangement in any such case with the rightful owner.

Chapter One: Domestic Violence

What is domestic violence?, © Women's Aid, *Myths and stereotypes*, © End the Fear, *How common is domestic abuse?*, © British Medical Association, *FAQs: why doesn't she leave?*, © Women's Aid, *Domestic abuse – my story*, © Lone Parents, *Domestic abuse 'epidemic' affects 8m*, © Telegraph Group Ltd, *Pregnant, but not immune from violence*, © iVillage UK, *Male victims of domestic violence*, © TheSite.org, *Domestic abuse in same-sex relationships*, © University of Bristol, *Same-gender abuse*, © Metropolitan Police Service, *Spyware: another weapon for domestic abuse*, © The Register, *Forced marriage*, © Manchester City Council, *Zena's story*, © Women's Aid.

Chapter Two: Abuse and Young People

Impact of domestic violence on children, © UNICEF, *Children and domestic violence*, © End the Fear, *'I loved and hated my father then; I love and hate him still'*, © Guardian Newspapers Ltd, *Domestic violence statistics*, © NSPCC, *Gender violence among teenagers*, © Amnesty International UK.

Chapter Three: Tackling Abuse

Options for domestic violence victims, © Citizens Advice, *Seeking help*, © University of Sheffield, *When violence first hit home*, © Guardian Newspapers Ltd, *Information for perpetrators*, © Men's Advice Line (MALE), *Pledge to cut domestic violence 'has failed'*, © Guardian Newspapers Ltd, *Rise in domestic violence convictions*, © Crown copyright is reproduced with the permission of Her Majesty's Stationery Office, *So what's the point of going to court?*, © Guardian Newspapers Ltd, *Domestic violence register called for*, © Emergency Services News.

Photographs

Flickr: pages 13 (Alice Hardman); 24 (Ingrid); 38 (Billogs).
Richard Owen: page 19.
Stock Xchng: pages 7 (Iris Alejandra Avendaño Acero); 9 (Cherie Wren); 12 (Nara Vieira da Silva Osga); 22 (Kat Callard); 32 (Kiel Latham).
Samantha Woolf: page 2.

Illustrations

Pages 1, 18, 35: Angelo Madrid; pages 3, 27: Bev Aisbett; pages 6, 21, 36: Simon Kneebone; pages 14, 23, 39: Don Hatcher.

Research and glossary by Claire Owen, with additional by Lisa Firth, on behalf of Independence Educational Publishers.

Additional editorial by Claire Owen, on behalf of Independence Educational Publishers.

And with thanks to the team: Mary Chapman, Sandra Dennis, Claire Owen and Jan Sunderland.

Lisa Firth
Cambridge
April, 2008